Carolyn G. Heilbrun

THE LAST GIFT

 *of*

TIME

Life Beyond

Sixty

Ballantine Books · New York

A Ballantine Book
Published by The Ballantine Publishing Group

http://www.randomhouse.com

Library of Congress Catalog Card Number: 98-96082

ISBN: 0-345-42295-3

This edition published by arrangement with Dial Press, an imprint of Dell Publishing, a division of Bantam Doubleday Dell Publishing Group, Inc.

Manufactured in the United States of America

Cover design by Ruth Ross
Designed by Francesca Belanger

First Ballantine Books Edition: May 1998

10   9   8   7

To Susan Heath
of New York, Staatsburg, London

Contents

Where are the songs of Spring? Ay, where are they?
Think not of them, thou hast thy music too.

—JOHN KEATS, "To Autumn"

THE LAST GIFT

of

TIME

PREFACE

Since [nature] has fitly planned the other acts of life's drama, it is not likely that she has neglected the final act as if she were a careless playwright.

—CICERO, *De Senectute*

LOOKING BACK, I can now perceive myself, a woman already in her sixties, engrossed in the question of what alterations in her life a woman might undertake upon turning fifty. In my writings, my public remarks, and my daily cogitations, I had concentrated on how a woman might best contemplate the start of a decade I had long since passed. This turning point of fifty, I had become convinced, ought to form as vital a milestone in a woman's life as graduation, promotion, marriage, or the birth or adoption of a child. At fifty, I had concluded, a woman might celebrate a rite of passage, a ritual as regularly marked as a confirmation. Trying to develop a ritual for this crossroads—the point at which a woman has lived thirty years of adult life in one mode and must discover a new mode for the second thirty years likely to be granted her—I wanted to suggest, to (if I am honest) urge women to see this new life as different, as a beginning, as a time requiring the questioning of all previous habits and activities, as, inevitably, a time of profound change.

When I was already sixty-two, I published *Writing a Woman's Life,* a work in which I proposed that female lives be looked at differently than had been customary for those writing biographies of women, or for women writing autobiographies, or for women looking anew at their own lives. I mused not only on aging but on friendship, marriage, and the gambits women used to escape a conventional and defining life, maneuvers of which the motive was often unconscious. Later, in articles and speeches, I suggested that aging might be gain rather than loss, and that the impersonation of youth was unlikely to provide the second span of womanhood with meaning and purpose.

What I had scarcely considered at all was the decade I was myself just passing through, the sixties. I, who had thought only of the rite of passage at fifty, have now discovered, at seventy, that the past ten years, the years of my sixties, were in their turn notably rewarding. (I am, of course, aware that my perspective is that of someone who has enjoyed many advantages. I have had a privileged education, worked for over thirty years as a professor of English at Columbia University before my retirement, and now enjoy a comfortable income. At the moment of recording this, I am in good health.) I was savoring a combination of serenity and activity that had hardly been publicly attributed, at least as far as I could discern, to women in their seventh decade. There seemed to be few accounts depicting the pleasures of this time of life. More familiar as an account of turning seventy was Doris Grumbach's *Coming into the End Zone,* a beautifully written journal about reaching her seventieth birthday that was a cry of despair and disillusion. She hated her aging body, she feared the streets of her city, she bemoaned the deaths of many beloved friends, and she created the impression, engraved on her narrative by her graceful, exact prose, that the better part of life had passed.

Her sixties, it was clear, had led inevitably to this moment of disillusion. Why were my sixties different? Why were those years, against all prognoses, worthy of commemoration? Grumbach and I share certain biographical details: We both grew up on the Upper West Side in Manhattan, the children of humanistic Jews; we both went to summer camps; we both had expensive educations. We had both married and had children, she four, I three; we both have grandchildren. At seventy, we were both living with longtime partners. We share certain quirks endemic to our age: an aversion to movies made from great novels, to ethnic food, travel, the doom-calls of dental hygienists, and women made over by plastic surgery, and a (daily) devotion to Progresso minestrone for lunch. And there, perhaps providing a clue to our different states of mind on reaching seventy, the similarities end. We have, as far as I remember, never met, although our mutual friend, the writer May Sarton, had offered us a tenuous connection.

Our differences are significant. Grumbach is a famous critic, in both print and television; she has many writer friends, from this profession and from the writers' colonies MacDowell and Yaddo; she is an intimate of renowned writers; she was beautiful and a devoted swimmer. Almost all the friends and writers she mentions are men; with the exception of an admired woman professor who influenced her in college, Grumbach leaves the impression of life full of male companionship and collegiality.

My sixties seemed to me, despite the usual setbacks and unkindnesses, so much luckier and more auspicious than Grumbach's that I felt impelled to seek the reason. That she suffered from deafness was not the answer: that condition, as she presented it, seemed almost a blessing to her in these noisy times. The most obvious difference was that I had acquired, in my late fifties and sixties, after a lifetime of solitude and few close and constant companions, women friends and colleagues, themselves now mature adults, whose intimacy helped to make the sixties my happiest decade. The men friends I had, all longtime familiars since graduate school, continued their welcome conversations; it was the newly befriended women, however, who made the significant difference for me.

Perhaps I am one of those who are born (as someone, probably Oscar Wilde, is said to have remarked of Max Beerbohm) blessed with the gift of eternal old age. If, like the poet Philip Larkin, I now appear to have been born aspiring to the age of sixty, I did not, like him, perceive that age as doom. Alan Bennett wrote of him: "Apparently [Larkin] is sixty, but when was he anything else? He has made a habit of being sixty, he has made a profession of it . . . he has been sixty for the last twenty-five years." As Larkin's biographer, Andrew Motion, observed about Larkin's sixtieth birthday, "Every word of praise told him his work was a thing of the past. Every mention of his birthday was a reminder of mortality." William Styron, writing of his terrible bout with depression, noted that it began at age sixty, "that hulking milestone of mortality." Is it death he fears, or age, or the loss of talent?

Depression weighs upon Grumbach as she contemplates the death of so many young men from AIDS, a despair echoed in these lines from Marilyn Hacker's "Against Elegies":

My old friends, my new friends who are old,
or older, sixty, seventy, take pills
with meals or after dinner. Arthritis
scourges them. But irremediable night is
farther away from them; they seem to hold
it at bay better than the young-middle-aged
whom something, or another something, kills
before the chapter's finished, the play staged.
The curtains stay down when the light fades. . . .

The sixty-five-year-olds are splendid, vying
with each other in work hours and wit.
They bring their generosity along,
setting the tone, or not giving a shit.

How well, or how eccentrically, they dress!
Their anecdotes are to the point, or wide
enough to make room for discrepancies.
But their children are dying.

The young and middle-aged in Hacker's poem are
dead or dying. And yet, the human irony is that those
of us who have reached seventy are rarely grateful:
since we did not wish to die, surely we must have
wished to grow old? But, ill-satisfied, we tend to sneer
at our flabby bodies and the inevitable fate that
dumped old age upon us. We do not remember, as
English writer Vera Brittain read in *The Pink Fairy
Book,* that Destiny offers the choice of happy youth or
happy old age, and that the choice of a happy youth is
not always the wiser one.

May Sarton, in her journal *At Seventy,* remarks on
having been asked to speak on old age at a Connecti-
cut college. In the course of her talk she said: "This is
the best time of my life. I love being old." A voice
from the audience demanded: "Why is it good to be
old?" As Sarton recounts it:

I answered spontaneously and a little on the defensive,
for I sensed incredulity in the questioner, "Because I am
more myself than I have ever been. There is less conflict. I am happier, more balanced, and" (I heard myself
say rather aggressively) "more powerful." I felt it was
rather an odd word, "powerful," but I think it is true. It
might have been more accurate to say "I am better able

to use my powers." I am surer of what my life is about, have less self-doubt to conquer.

Turning seventy, enjoying what W. H. Auden (who, however, did not live to that age) called "obesity and a little fame," I found the revelation that I could look back upon my sixties with pleasure astonishing. Having supposed the sixties would be downhill all the way, I had long held a determination to commit suicide at seventy. Yet for a time the fact that my sixties had offered such satisfactions only confirmed my lifelong resolution not to live past "threescore years and ten." Quit while you're ahead was, and is, my motto.

I had always considered this biblical life span to be a highly reasonable one. Having reached my seventieth year, I did not at once search for reasons to question its veracity. True, my life was good. But is it not better to leave at the height of well-being rather than contemplate the inevitable decline and the burden one becomes upon others? I have always been a lonely person, given to mild melancholy from time to time. But I had never before, however gloomy, seriously contemplated suicide; that was an option permissible, for myself, only at seventy. Now, turning seventy, I recalled a snatch of conversation from an Ivy Compton-Burnett novel. One of the characters says: "Cassius was not of an age to die." "What is the age?" her sister asks. "About seventy," a brother answers, "when we have had our span, and people have not begun to think the less of us." Well, I thought, that's where I am.

Of course, when I long ago settled upon the determination to end my life at seventy, that age seemed far off, indeed unlikely ever to occur. As William Hazlitt said, "No young man ever thinks he shall die"—and no young woman either. I had even mentioned this resolution to my children, who began nervously to inquire about my thoughts on the general subject of death when that monumental seventieth birthday came around. I seemed so thriving that, I am sure, they were not seriously concerned; the young and even the happily mature often resolve to avoid old age, changing their views as what they had dismissed as "old age" arrives. They continue to find life precious, though disabilities accumulate.

Even the Bible hedges a bit. I looked up the phrase "threescore years and ten" in the concordance to the Bible that belonged to my mother (who had acquired it for the solving of crossword puzzles and Double-Crostics); the concordance directed me to Psalm 90, whose tenth verse reads: "The days of our years are threescore years and ten; and if by reason of strength they be fourscore years, yet is their strength labour and sorrow; for it is soon cut off and we fly away." The psalm proclaims throughout the uselessness of human life, but the assurance that an extra ten years avail one nothing was, I thought, particularly sound.

In short, I had, despite the unexpected pleasures of my recently concluded sixties, begun to contemplate ending my life, taking seriously the advice of Dorothy Sayers's famous detective Lord Peter Wimsey to his nephew, St. George: "If you insist on blowing out your brains, do it in someplace where you will not cause mess and inconvenience." Lord Peter was being facetious, but the advice was nonetheless proper. Perhaps beginning myself to doubt my determination, I mentioned the problem to a friend I could trust not to go all silly at my discussion of suicide. Since I am, as I dare say is evident, a rather unconventional person, and since most women and men of my generation are highly conventional and become more so with the passing of years, I have tended to cultivate friendships with younger women. This friend was one of the more enduring.

"What about waiting to see how it goes?" she asked on this occasion.

"The trouble with that," I said, "and it is a very tempting approach to the problem, is that by the time you really know you want to die you are too weak, or powerless, or ill to do anything about it."

"I take your point," she said. One of the things I like about this friend is that she does take points without endless toing-and-froing. "But surely one can compromise without waiting for total ineptitude."

"I think what I have in mind will only work if a specific date is set," I said. "It's leaving the party while it's still fun. I know, I don't like parties and neither do you, but it's the best metaphor I can come up with."

My friend smiled. "Why not compromise on the Bible's two mentioned dates: make it seventy-five. After all, surely one lives longer these days, healthily, I mean; those of us born to privilege get good starts in life, inoculations, vaccinations, antibiotics, that sort of thing."

"I've considered seventy-five," I said. "But right now seventy seems to me the right age, the right moment."

As is evident from the fact that I am writing this, I did not choose death at seventy. I was—and am—one of those for whom work is the essence of life. German artist Käthe Kollwitz, when she was old, noticed that her work had become independent of the events in her life. "The readiness forms in waves inside myself," she said. "I need only be on the alert for when the tide at last begins to rise again." And in me, the tide had begun to rise.

I find it powerfully reassuring now to think of life as "borrowed time." Each day one can say to oneself: I can always die; do I choose death or life? I daily choose life the more earnestly because it is a choice. There is the famous story of Alice James, the younger sister of William and Henry, with four older brothers and the confinements of a nineteenth-century female destiny: still young, she asked her father for permission to commit suicide and he, wise man, gave it to her. She chose to live. I, with the same permission given by myself, also choose, each day for now, to live.

THE SMALL HOUSE

> a toft-and-croft
> where I needn't, ever, be at home *to*
>
> those I am not at home *with* . . .
> not a windowless grave, but a place
> I may go both in and out of.
>
> —W. H. AUDEN, *"Thanksgiving for a Habitat"*

WHEN I WAS SIXTY-EIGHT I bought a house. "But we already have a house," my husband pointed out, for he had long suspected that I was searching less for a house than for solitude.

Solitude, late in life, is the temptation of the happily paired; to be alone if one has not been doomed to aloneness is a temptation so beguiling that it carries with it the guilt of adultery, and the promise of consummation. Men have long taken themselves off to business, their health club, who knew where, more often than not leaving women far from alone—with children, with the fulfillment of daily necessities, or, worst of all, with an obsession for a man who is not there and does not call. "If to be left were to be left alone," Edna St. Vincent Millay wrote, "And lock the door and find one's self again"—this is the ideal, but if the woman is unwillingly alone, "neither with you nor with my self, I spend / Loud days that have no meaning and no end." To find one's self again, or to find a new self, leads many a woman—Anne Morrow Lindbergh, Alix Kates Shulman, Doris Grumbach—to a wish for a period of solitude, but paired, they return, after the allotted span of seclusion, to love, and domestic duties, and the comforting routine of the shared life.

By the end of my sixties, I had come to understand that there was a rift in my life that I had not earlier identified: between country solitude and city solitude. There was never any question of my living the usual city life, with evenings devoted to partaking of the performing arts, to dinner parties, to museum attendance at blockbuster exhibits, to vacations devoted to travel. Occasional solitude was what I sought, country solitude, the house to which one might flee, probably on weekends, to invite one's soul and encounter peace. New York was where I had my being, where I was even now sometimes alone. I needed a solitude away from the city, even as I would return there with happiness and relief. Arnold Bennett, the English novelist, is supposed to have remarked that the best part of a weekend in the country was the 4:52 back to London.

The house we already owned, and had owned for twenty-five years—large, rambling, and set in unnecessary abundance of acres—embodied the dreams of my early adulthood, the setting for family life that I, an only city child, had read of and innocently longed for. Near a farm, redolent of cows, backed (with absurd literalness) by amber waves of grain in the adjacent field, and boasting a rushing brook, this house was, when we bought it, in disrepair, but full, as we continued over the years to point out to each other, of possibilities. In the many summers of family "togetherness"—a buzzword of that supposedly idyllic, actually wretched time—I kept distant from consciousness the fact that I cared for none of it, not the hikes, or the guests, or the meals, or the gossipy neighbors. I was coming on sixty before I could acknowledge that that particular house was not for me, a recognition that occurred simultaneously with two of our children's discovery that it was, of all possible places, the most beloved.

My husband concurred in their devotion. We had improvidently acquired the house and two mortgages (five percent each) because my husband's boyhood summers—filled with what he remembered as a joyous childhood in a rural commune—had been nearby. Perhaps he hoped to re-create it, but he had, for this purpose, married the wrong woman. I took neither to cooking, gardening, repairing, nor the welcoming of guests. It could be said with accuracy that in all this (to its visitors) splendid rural experience, I delighted not: I endured.

In recent years two of our children, together with their friends, lovers, and, eventually, spouses, have rushed joyfully to the house on every weekend and vacation, filling it with the sounds of family life so dear to sitcoms: slamming screen doors, shouts from ground to high window, outdoor cooking and drinking, the litter of youth. I became inspired: we will divide the house, I said. It was large enough for this, comprising two staircases and many small rooms. Our son Robert, who, following his graduation from college, had worked for a subcontractor, constructed a dividing wall and a second kitchen. But division did not bring serenity to me: their cats fought with our cat, the voices still cheerfully rang, their intermittent hospitality engulfed us. My husband, equipped from birth with an ever-ready carapace, was able to work anywhere, emerging happily at the day's end to marvel at the light on the fields and the amber waves of grain. Little by little, he took to going to the country without me. The children invited him to their always sumptuous, many-personed dinners; otherwise, satisfactorily armored, he labored alone, occasionally exhilarated by the vigorous hike he could sometimes induce his children to undertake.

Then I secretly decided to buy a house of my own, where no person (not even the nearest and dearest) and no demand would intrude on my seclusion. True, I had found solitude in our New York apartment during his country weekends, but some change of scene, I began to suspect, was necessary as counterpoint to my daily urban existence. But I emphatically did not want ramshackle rural counterpoint. I wanted a house altogether different from my youthful sitcom dream, indeed its exact opposite. My house would be less than two hours from New York, small, modern, full of machinery that *worked*, and above all habitable in winter, so that I might sit in front of a fire and contemplate, meditate, conjure, and, if in need of distraction, read.

My desires are few, but once identified, insistent; we set off at once upon the search. (It never occurred to me to search alone: it would be my house, but I wanted spousal reassurances about the structural soundness of my investment.) I am fortunate in that I have seemed never to wish for what I could not afford. And, with ample pensions and savings, we are what used to be called "comfortable." This, the costliest of my desires, happily followed upon the close of our children's expensive education.

Communing with a map—a talent I have never acquired—my husband identified an area just too far for commuters (our other house was three hours from the City), with taxes not too elevated, in a school district not too sought after. I didn't care, I cavalierly remarked, if my house had little or no land, if it had close neighbors, if it was in a town, if it had no view; none of that mattered, I assured my husband, as long as the house promised minimal upkeep, insulation, and rational machinery. (Our other house has a water-heating system and a thermostat—not to mention the roof or the cellar or the refrigerator or the stopped-up sinks—that not only demand attention but inevitably become the constant subject of what passes in those parts for conversation.) I astonished my by-this-time-impervious husband by adding that I particularly did not want beautiful old trees. We had magnificent ancient sugar maples at the other house; they died, they lost limbs, they collapsed in unexpected storms. I loved them and they threatened to break my heart. I didn't, in short, want to love this new house; I wanted merely to exist in it, alone, contemplating saplings, soothed by the purr of functioning appliances.

My desire and subsequent search for a house was destined, I later realized to befuddle everyone who heard of it. I began by astonishing the affable real estate agent: I did not, I informed him, want a swimming pool. But, he said, everyone wants a swimming pool. I don't, I assured him, I never swim. And those I know of with pools are always either closing them or opening them, or fencing them, or cleaning them. No pool. He had to study his available properties with extreme care to find a modern house without a pool, even for what we could spend.

I saw my dream retreat on the first day we dashed about—mostly viewing modern imitations of colonial houses. It had been hopefully built twenty years ago as a barn destined to be turned by someone into a dwelling. A perfectly square building with a large window evoking a hayloft, this new, cowless barn stood for some time, like a beached and deserted ship, on a windy hill. The builder camped out in the back of his unsold barn, waiting; then, in the 1980s, a couple, enraptured and challenged, bought the barn and designed an inside. They left a huge living room, with a neat kitchen attached; above, with balconies that looked down on the living room, was an only slightly smaller bedroom with a cathedral ceiling. There was wood everywhere but on the contrasting white walls. The cellar was neat, the three bathrooms were up-to-date—including the ordained Jacuzzi that I, who never take tub baths, was prepared to ignore.

We saw other houses, including charming old wrecks yearning to be "fixed up." (The real estate agent was experienced enough to know how many people, determined upon modern houses, fall in love with something they could magnificently transform. I shook my head firmly.) We went away and returned. My less impulsive husband persuaded me that there was sense in continuing to look. But I knew in that stark wooden rectangle on a windy hill I had found what I wanted. No one knew or was saying what had become of the former owners who had so meticulously constructed the barn's inside, but a representative of the IRS, vigilantly present at the closing, suggested unhappy circumstances.

Ironically, the house that was now mine came with five acres and a long view of a two-hundred-acre Christmas tree farm rising beyond the property line. The other neighbor, a corporate officer, had just completed landscaping his new home, elegant with ponds and wide lawns resembling a Jane Austen park wherein walked the ladies—a balm to the spirit. He and his gracious wife allowed me to wander there, admiring a vista both natural and designed. The cultivator of

Christmas trees similarly allowed me to tramp across his fields. The few who stopped by for a visit could rarely see in the house what I saw, but the serendipity of those surrounding acres, infinitely tempting to one whose only exercise was walking, was evident to all.

The first weekend after its purchase, I drove to my new place of solitude accompanied by my husband, who would then take the car on to the other house, an additional hour distant from New York. He would stop for me on his way home; fair enough.

"Perhaps I better show you how the furnace works," he said as we carried in my supplies. A bed had been delivered previously, and we had earlier brought two folding deck chairs from the other house. He put the pots, dishes, and various other equipment down on the counter and suggested a tour of the cellar.

"The hot water heater is on a timer," he said. "It's a little complicated; be sure to wear rubber gloves if you want to put it on manual or change the timer."

"Where is it?" I asked.

He looked at me. "The engineer showed us," he said. We went to the cellar to examine the furnace and the timer for the water heater. I didn't understand why it needed a timer, but I didn't ask. We returned to the living room.

"Well," he said, "I'm off. Call if you want anything."

We had had a phone installed; I had the necessary

provisions, easily enough for my minimal requirements.

"Make a list of the things you find you need," he said. "After all, I'm leaving you without a car, so you have to plan a bit carefully."

And he left.

There is, as Millay knew, alone and alone. I loved the pine, and the white walls, and the space, and the quiet, and soon I would have a comfortable chair and a reading lamp and a computer. . . . I wandered around the rooms, becoming acquainted. There were light switches all over the house; I tried them all, and hoped to remember what they ignited. Eventually, I heated a can of soup for my lunch and began to make a list of necessary tools, furnishings, and supplies. Solitude, ironically enough, seems to begin with an awareness of what one will require while alone. I doubt that anyone, undertaking a spell of solitude, will not consider her needs in far more detail than were she setting out for a companioned stay. (About the only thing the about-to-be solitary does not agonize over is clothes.)

Somehow, I found it hard to settle. Sitting on one of the deck chairs in the middle of the enormous living room, I contemplated my domain. The white walls, with windows interspersed, reminded me of a ballet studio. I intended to put no pictures on the walls; I wanted it like this: stark, unadorned, comfortable. But I could not seem to settle. I opened the bottle of wine that the real estate agent had thoughtfully left with a welcoming note, priding myself on having remembered to bring my Swiss Army knife with its corkscrew.

Under one of the kitchen cabinets a mouse stirred. I had tried to prepare myself for this. An animal lover embracing all species—I believe with William Blake that everything that lives is holy—I had inherited from my mother, who had it from her mother, a horror of mice skittering across a floor. Unlike my mother, who had been known to leave a movie theater when a mouse appeared on the screen, I held the creatures willingly in a laboratory or pet store but could not readily accustom myself to sharing indoor space with a rampant rodent. Country solitude demanded that I overcome this inherited repulsion, but the effort to do so did not easily convey itself to my nervous system. I made further inroads on the bottle of wine. Eventually, I went upstairs to the lovely bedroom which would also be my study, made the bed, lay down on top of it, and napped.

I was awakened by a pounding on the front door. Bewildered but not frightened—mice alone evoke terror in me—trying to smooth my hair and clothes, I descended to encounter, I was reasonably sure, Jehovah's Witnesses. My husband stood on the doorstep.

"I thought maybe I should keep you company, just for the first night," he said. I could not remember ever having been so happy to see him, at least not since his ship had docked following World War II. "It's not a precedent," he assured me.

In the fullness of time, as they used to say, my

house acquired two comfortable chairs and two reading lamps—one for my husband, should he find himself, for whatever unforeseen reason, spending some time there. I bought a desk to put in the bedroom and a computer to put on the desk. I have always preferred my surroundings to be tidy and simple, and so they were. Watching over us, as though the totem and guardian of the house, was a benign, smiling gargoyle of molded stone, sent by our daughter Emily. This gargoyle came with a sweetly appropriate story:

It all began in Paris when the Notre Dame Cathedral was being built, rising majestically stone by stone toward the heavens. It was custom to top each structure with a menacing gargoyle, who protected the cathedral by warding off evil spirits. Marie Therese, a nun from a tiny convent in Provence, disliked the evil-looking gargoyle on the new cathedral, sitting so close to the heavens. Disguised as a man, she trekked on foot to Paris, entered the worksite, and quickly carved a small block into a lovable, protective creature. She placed her creature, with its pointy ears and human-like feet, on the highest roof, visible only to God Himself.

How did all this happen? I have thought back, pondering about solitude and long marriages, and the strange tilting of our desires. My husband went to the other house, but, he said, it wasn't the same without me. He had been, I hardly needed to point out, happy enough there when I stayed in New York. Weren't the children company? Yes, he didn't know the reason, but if I was in a country house, he wanted to be in that country house. Of course, he would always spend time at the old house, that went without saying. Meanwhile. . . .

My happiness at having him with me continued—driving up and down with me, working at the built-in desk just off the living room, monitoring the machinery, conferring with the man who mows the lawn and sells us wood, and sitting on the chair with the lamp and table we had together chosen beside him. I thought, perhaps it was not solitude I had wanted, but a simpler country life, sparser furnishings, a house in which the only noise was mine and his.

We had lived together for close to half a century, and if I lacked solitude, as assuredly I did for most of that time, it was not because he intruded upon my desire to be alone. I had to face it, I wasn't up to the mechanics of even a modern, recently equipped house. I didn't want to work outside, cutting bushes, encouraging grass, or planting petunias for the hummingbirds. I might want a country house, but I wasn't equipped to manage one, nor to build the screens he constructed for the big French doors in the living room, allowing us to take advantage of the breezes on our windy hill. I wanted to prove I could be a woman alone, and I had failed.

Suppose I had had no husband? Or suppose my husband had refused to have anything to do with this strange barn of a house? I like to believe I would have learned to manage, that I would have coped, that I could have discovered the use for all the tools he set up on the workbench in the cellar, and could have managed to use them, particularly the electric drill.

Perhaps, now, I might last in my new house, alone, solitary, if I had to. But could I have managed from the beginning? I doubt it. Those who seek solitude often mistake it, I suspect. They want it because they can leave it, because it is not their whole destiny. In New York I know I would make out all right, I would last. But to seek solitude in unaccustomed surroundings, or in temporary surroundings, is to go in search of a fantasy.

"I didn't want to be in the other house without you," he said. And yet during the day we sit now in "my" house, he down, I up, not talking for hours. Later, smiling across the large living room at each other as I tend the woodstove (at that I am wonderfully talented), we do not talk much, we read different books. In a sense, current events or the requirements of maintenance aside, there is not much to talk about. I think as a literary person, he as an economist restrained by data, hungry for statistics.

Ours is a long marriage, and we have found solitude together. But had I not followed a fantasy, we would not enjoy it now in this stark barn, where the wild turkeys come in groups to eat the corn we scatter on the snow, and the fire speaks to us of rural contentment.

THE DOG WHO CAME
TO STAY

I worry.
I have to because nobody else does. . . .
Who knows who it could be at the door
'Specially in these times. . . .
So I worry.
Sleep with my ears up, not soundly.
When I'm not watching I'm greeting.
People are not grateful enough
For visitors. I am. I worry
About them not being grateful enough. . . .
Between the dangers
And the greetings I'm simply exhausted.

—ARTHUR MILLER'S DOG LOLA, "Lola's Lament"

THE HUMANE SOCIETY of New York called her
Bianca, for what reason we never thought to ask. Perhaps they did not appreciate the oddness of naming a
black dog Bianca, or perhaps they were thinking, as we
later surmised, of Bianca Jagger. As Maxine Kumin
has observed, "the less pedigreed the dog the more
elegant the name." My husband and I thought of
changing her name, but we could not help wondering
how many names she had had in her life. Bianca was

her name when we met her, and so Bianca she remained.

Two years before we returned to the Humane Society for a dog, we had lost Toby, the cat I had adopted from there. Toby was a Maine coon cat, the child of divorce; I had found him one afternoon when, unable to live without an animal, I had on impulse visited the Humane Society, from which one of our children had recently adopted a cat. Toby was not his Humane Society name—they called him Trix, highly unsuitable, he was a wonderfully dignified cat—and we immediately renamed him Toby, after Uncle Toby in *Tristram Shandy*. He lived with us for twelve years, finally falling, in the country, victim—or so we guessed—to a coyote. I would have liked a dog even then, when I adopted Toby, but as a working couple we could not possibly consider a dog, who would have been alone all day. The dog we had had when the children were growing up had lived to sixteen, and in the end, with the children at college and both of us gone every day, we were hardly able to care for her and had to farm her out.

My need for a dog presented itself to me as an inarguable fact. When accounting for this sudden, unquenchable longing, I managed to marshal a few sensible arguments: I was not getting out enough, never, for example, walking in the summer heat; if I stayed alone in the small house, as I had never done in the older house, I would feel safer with a dog; a large, fierce-seeming dog would enable me really to explore

Central Park, as I had not done since childhood in those less dangerous times. No doubt there were other reasons, fabricated at the time and now quite forgotten, but these reasons, at least, endured; Bianca made them all into the facts of our lives, hers and mine. The simple truth, however, was that I desired a dog, as Elizabeth Barrett Browning put it in quite other connections, "with a passion put to use in my old griefs, and with my childhood's faith." Was it that I had never had a dog in my childhood, though I had longed for one with an intensity that troubled my parents (but not enough for action in the matter)? I do not, all the same, support the view that turns exclusively to childhood for the explanations of adult desires, and in any case, I experienced my need for canine companionship suddenly, as a compulsion, a necessity of my sixties.

But this time, I did not let the impulse carry me alone to the Humane Society. For one thing, I could not have a dog without the cooperation of my husband, who, honesty suggested, would be the one to take her on her short, early morning outing. Rising before the morning is well advanced is difficult for me, and when, for various scheduling reasons, I am forced to get up early, I am groggy and out of sorts for most of the day. But even beyond this morning task, the acquisition of a dog demands more fundamental agreement by those who live together than does a cat; cats, if one is not a loather of the feline species, can be largely ignored.

Also, I knew that if I went to the Humane Society alone, or even accompanied, I could not come home empty-handed, but would inevitably return with a dog, and not necessarily a dog in accordance with my requirements. My husband, therefore, agreed to scout out the situation first, without me. We had decided on a German shepherd, or at least a German shepherd type dog. (Clio, our earlier dog, had been the result of the unplanned union of a boxer and the German shepherd next door; she was the best dog ever.)

There were, it transpired, several German shepherds available, including one female, Bianca, whom the attendant was pushing; he liked her and wanted her to have a home. Together we visited the German shepherds the next day. There was a magnificent male named Kaiser, who had been adopted as a puppy seven years ago from the Humane Society and had, on the death of his owner, returned. Only spousal firmness wrenched me from consideration of Kaiser. "Are you out of your mind?" was the way my husband delicately put it. "He won't even fit in our car."

We returned to contemplation of Bianca. Where Kaiser had been a magnificent example of the breed, she looked like a valiant attempt at a German shepherd that had fallen short. Every aspect of her was not quite right; yet there was no question of what breed she had aspired to join. She was totally black, except for her tan legs; one ear stood up, the other folded over. She sat for the attendant, who assured us that she was not only housebroken but trained to obey many commands; this training, as we later confirmed, had not always been kind. Her history was vague—the Humane Society offers only the strictly medical in its reports, rather like an old-fashioned adoption agency. Someone had found her roaming the streets, had paid a substantial bill to restore her to health, and had gained her admission to the Humane Society.

We took her home; they provided a collar and leash. I had planned to walk, a good hike from far east on Fifty-ninth Street to the West Side of Manhattan, which I had thought would cement our relationship. But the Society dissuaded us. We must take a taxi, they said; dogs leaving the Humane Society might get overexcited walking home, pull loose and be lost. The young attendant found us a taxi. I got in, and Bianca, all sixty-something pounds of her, got in on my lap. My husband sat beside us, talking to the driver to alleviate his misgivings about his canine passenger.

Was it in that moment, leaning against me in the taxi, held by my arms, that she decided I was the person around whom the rest of her life would revolve? Partly, we eventually decided, she had been mistreated by a man. She has remained more suspicious of men than women; while she came immediately to recognize my husband as a member of our pack, and accepted other men as friends, if met frequently, she greeted familiar women with unalloyed joy. Once home, she stayed beside me, indoors and out: if I went from one room to another, she would get up and follow me. It was only when she had been with us for almost two years that she would leave me working in my study in the late evening to go into the bedroom to lie on her bed from L. L. Bean.

The Humane Society had said she was three to four years old. We soon realized that she was five, at least. I was glad of this: I did not want a youthful dog, I wanted a serious and dignified adult dog, a little stiff, perhaps, like me upon arising, but vigorous and attentive. She was too attentive, really. In the country, she begged me to go for walks, but would not so much as step outside without me. When I went away, which I tended to do less and less once Bianca had come to stay, she turned her attention to my husband as substitute and promise. No one who has not, upon returning from any absence, long or short, been greeted by a loving dog can understand what devotion is. There is no affection like it available anywhere else on earth, and those for whom it is the heart's balm, as it is for me, understand what a love elixir is—one that never, as it does so often for humans, fails to work both ways. Rudyard Kipling understood this:

> Day after day, the whole day through—
> Wherever my road inclined—
> Four-Feet said "I am coming with you!"
> And trotted along behind.

There are many lost and abandoned dogs in this country. We, who are shocked that in some cultures people eat dogs, seem not to care how many we are forced to put to death. I have all my life been haunted by abandoned dogs running along the highway, peering into every car in the forlorn hope that their owners have come back for them. To adopt one dog makes no great change in the expanse of cruelty increasing daily, but one dog at least is saved. Mark Twain is supposed to have said that the difference between taking in a dog and a man is that the dog will not bite you. Anyone who has adopted a lost dog will tell you that the dog is, quite evidently, grateful. It is said that greyhounds, no longer able to run in races, are the most grateful; any life after the one they have led is paradise.

Bianca had been beaten—for the first few months she flinched whenever we suddenly put out a hand—and she had clearly been alone in the city; she had scavenged. We could tell this because she still retained the talent for smelling out food however invisible or unappealing to our eyes. We learned that the sign of spring was chicken bones abandoned under park benches from take-out lunches, and we became watchful. Outdoors she would fall into old scavenging ways; indoors she was courtesy itself, reminding us of mealtime or walk time with the gentlest of nudges.

We were sometimes asked why we didn't adopt a dog in the country, as we had done with our first dog. But we got Clio as a puppy, and brought her to the city for the first time when she was only a few months old. A grown dog, unaccustomed to city noises, to sirens, traffic, the subway, the screams of crowds of children, the roar of buses, would, I feared, be terrified. Bianca had heard it all before. I guessed, from the way she glanced all about her before crossing a street, even with me on the other end of her leash, that she had crossed on her own and taken account of what cars could do. The city did not alarm her; she was a city dog, as I was a city person.

But how do you travel if you have a dog? I was asked. Where do you leave her? We all operate from unconscious or unexamined reasons as well as conscious, clearly stated ones. I do not like to travel. I have never been a sightseer, never understood the attraction of having been somewhere, taken pictures, had the sights pointed out, and then returning to inflict the details of your journey upon acquaintances. Not that I defend this decidedly eccentric opinion; it is a lifelong quirk, and after one extended sight-seeing tour of Europe in my early twenties, I have rarely traveled, except upon invitation to speak or the chance to visit those living in another country. The remarks of everyone I know who enjoys travel—which is to say everyone I know—have long made clear the oddness of my dislike. From my husband, a devoted traveler, has come a slow understanding of my disinclinations and acceptance of them. He travels alone, or with a friend. I have, furthermore, discovered that for those in their sixties and long married, separate trips are a chance to be oneself, to acquire, through the temporary detachment travel can offer, a fresh view of marital life together.

Bianca, in impeding my chances for leisurely

travel, posed no threat. I do have invitations to speak from across the country, however, and while I have always found that these trips provide valuable experiences, the discomfort of air travel, of getting to the New York airports, of waiting for delayed takeoffs, of sitting in the dreadfully uncomfortable, inadequate airplane seats provided, has become, if not torture, close to it. Bianca's presence in my life would make me consider such trips more closely and refuse them more often. I may not have allowed my knowledge of that fact to emerge into consciousness. But conscious or not, the knowledge was certainly no deterrent to acquiring her.

I have become more physically settled in my sixties, liking to be home, or toggling from one home to the next. Routine, which I used to scorn as next door to incarceration, holds new appeal for me. But one must not sit and think and ruminate all day. And so, with Bianca, I walk one hour every day, rain or shine, snow or sleet, cold or hot; that hour is unavoidable. As I like to point out, a dog is the only exercise machine you cannot decide to skip when you don't feel like it. The houses of my friends and acquaintances are cluttered with exercise machines that often sit ignored, collecting dust, during the stresses of life. But late every morning, however I am feeling, Bianca and I have our walk.

In walking, as in life, I have changed my pace. I used to hurry, always, and could scarcely tolerate those who ambled; to walk with the old or infirm was, quite literally, torture for me, although I tried not to show it. When one is working, when one's children are young, one must be efficient, one must hurry, one must get on with it. I enjoyed that pace, and am glad to have been what my mother used to call a peppy sort of person. Now, I saunter once in a while. Bianca and I do not rush across the street as the light is about to change; we wait for the next light, looking about us, seeing things. In the park, I meander, catching sight of what, years ago, I would not have noticed. Bianca, off the leash, stays nearby but covers more ground at a faster pace. It is, of course, illegal for her to be off the leash, and I keep an eye out for the park patrol people who will give you tickets. But she is well enough trained to come when called, and sufficiently, perhaps unduly, protective, so that she keeps an eye on me too. The occasional man, approaching suddenly to ask the directions or the time, has been momentarily frightened to have a large black dog run toward him, barking fiercely. Muggers avoid us. No one messes with me when Bianca and I are together.

Bianca has constrained my life, there is no doubt of that. I even find myself wondering if it is worth returning a book to the shelves in another room, knowing that as I move, she will move, and she is sleeping peacefully near to me. If my husband and I must both go out and leave her, I am sad, and picture her waiting for us to return, lying by the door, listening. I do not think I go out during the day as often as I used to, although I tell myself, with justice, that the afternoon is my working time. Perhaps if I did not have Bianca, I would accept more speaking engagements on days when my husband cannot be home. Perhaps I would live differently, without Bianca.

There is no commitment that does not bring with it its own tensions, and its own ambivalences. Bianca, lying beside me as I write, has had her costs, but she fulfills a need I did not earlier believe I had, and whose depth I have been astonished to discover. As Sartre said, not to choose is to have already chosen. The major danger in one's sixties—so I came to feel—is to be trapped in one's body and one's habits, not to recognize those supposedly sedate years as the time to discover new choices and to act upon them. To continue doing what one had been doing—which was Dante's idea of hell—is, I came to see, and the vision frightened me, easy in one's sixties. In my case, a passionate need for a dog—and of course desires vary widely in range and intensity—was required to turn stability into action. An answer for most people certainly is not, as it was for me, to head for the Humane Society.

My desire for Bianca, and my pleasure in her, was rewarding, as many seemingly odd choices can be rewarding, if at a price. Of course there is always a price. But the fear of paying it, I convinced myself before giving in to my need for a dog, is the highest price of all.

TIME

Either you will
go through this door
or you will not go through.

If you go through
there is always the risk
of remembering your name.

Things look at you doubly
and you must look back
and let them happen.

If you do not go through
it is possible
to live worthily

to maintain your attitudes
to hold your position
to die bravely

but much will blind you,
much will evade you,
at what cost who knows?

The door itself
makes no promises.
It is only a door.

—ADRIENNE RICH, "Prospective Immigrants Please Note"

Doris Grumbach, in her recent book *Extra Innings,* echoes my thirty-year experience in academia, teaching English literature at Columbia University, when she reports on attending a Phi Beta Kappa committee meeting:

All the things I most disliked about academic meetings in the old days were present at this one: the fraudulent surface of civility, the undercurrent of prearranged and determined agendas, the rude disregard of a woman chairman by male members of the executive committee accustomed to dominating every occasion of their privileged lives, their loud (or contrivedly too-soft) and always obtrusive voices carrying every question and insisting on every answer. My humiture was intense. I came away feeling sick, tired, discouraged, and angry at myself for spending four days of my diminishing supply of time in this absurd way.

On the plane I decided to resign.

I have not been able to discover what "humiture" means, but the sense of being humiliated is certainly there somewhere. In any case, I, too, resigned.

The general attitude toward feminists in the English department at Columbia was nicely exemplified by one of its chief movers and shakers: when asked by the *Columbia Spectator* to name the ten worst books in his opinion, this "scholar" listed as his tenth choice "Any book of poems by Adrienne Rich (all deserve inclusion.)" For me and many others, of course, Adrienne Rich had been the most valiant of the early feminists, with daringly specific analyses of women's condition and the best enunciated vision of their possible future, both within and without the classroom. She was, in addition, a great poet, whose promise, before she blackened her name with feminism, had been proclaimed by W. H. Auden.

I was shocked, almost from the moment I left Columbia, by how little I missed it, how relieved I was not to have to plunge, ever again, into that poisonous atmosphere. I had the chance to stay in touch with some of my students whose dissertations I continued to sponsor, or who spoke with me upon occasion. But I thought now I understood how privileged Victorian women must have felt when they took off the stays and dresses that inhibited motion, and flexed their bodies, moved their unbound muscles. I had feared that I would miss the structure of teaching and the institutional base from which to make scholarly requests. True, my scholarly attention to criticism in my field wavered and, ultimately, faltered; I observed this with little regret. I entered upon a life unimagined previously, of happiness impossible to youth or to the years of being constantly needed both at home and at work. I entered into a period of freedom, and only past sixty learned in what freedom consists: to live without a constant, unnoticed stream of anger and resentment, without the daily contemplation of power always in the hands of the least worthy, the least imaginative, the least generous. Everyone I met commented on how well I looked, how relaxed, how glowing. Never having expected to retire, not having yet considered it before the need to quit came upon me, I discovered retirement to be a gift especially suited to my sixties, when I could best relish its delicate flavor.

And there was something else. I learned that while exiting—from a marriage, a job, a place, a family, or an institution—is always a possibility, it is an action undertaken only with great reluctance and dilatoriness in what is called "the prime of life." (The young often declare themselves, as they put it, "out of here," but that is a youthful habit that seldom endures.) Because I was in my sixties, I could exit without that action requiring great courage or troubling contemplation of no income or of empty years. Our sixties give us the chance to get out, not only from a job but from much else that we have been doing unquestioningly for a long time. I do not, for example, think that one should leave a marriage lightly, certainly not a long one. But I do think unless one is able to contemplate such a move, the marriage will not undergo changes necessary to the renewal of a long, habit-ridden relationship.

Having left my position at Columbia, I found myself enabled, encouraged, to consider all my alliances, family, social, professional, and to think especially about friendships. This may be why I was able, after such attention to the quality of comradeship, to enjoy more than ever the company of friends who had not known me forever and did not think themselves certain of what I was about. I was not eager to eliminate relationships or end associations, but rather to reassure myself that everything that was dictating the pattern of my life was both understood and, once understood, chosen again only after long reflection. I came to admit my intense discomfort with those who could converse only with a younger me. As Virginia Woolf put it with her usual elegance, "I don't want immaturities, things torn out of time, preserved, unless in some strong casket, with one key only."

In a famous speech from *The Winter's Tale* a young lover recounts his admiration:

> When you speak, sweet,
> I'd have you do it ever; when you sing,
> I'd have you buy and sell so; so give alms;
> Pray so; and for the ordering your affairs,
> To sing them too. When you do dance, I wish you
> A wave o' the sea, that you might ever do
> Nothing but that; move still, still so,
> And own no other function. Each your doing,
> So singular in each particular,
> Crowns what you are doing in the present deed,
> That all your acts are queens.

This exquisite paean of romantic love is rightly celebrated, and yet it is a male dream of woman which we women have internalized and which we must learn to refute. The ideal is not to be loved forever, to stay exactly as you are, "never never change," as the song has it. Of all the "rights" we women have sought, none is more difficult, or more vital, than the right to change, to cease doing it "ever." This is not to say that some of what we have been doing, reconsidered, will not still be worth the doing at sixty and beyond. But I found that habit, even beautiful and generous habit, even professional or marital habit, could become a killing monster, and could be defeated, after careful analysis, by the daring of abandonment.

But haven't we women always been abandoned, "seduced and abandoned," as the saying goes? Certainly. And old women have been left for younger women or for equally miserable and cowardly reasons. Fear of abandonment can, of course, leave an individual woman not only the victim of that very fear but, in her anxiety to hold on to the man she fears may take off, lost to herself. None of this is easy; the anger I felt, the nastiness I experienced, the resentment I felt toward Columbia were all there at first, even if my leaving was easier than most such exits or departures. But had I stayed, I would have lost the chance to take control of my own ideas of rightness, to do the hard thing.

The rare, delicate flavor of a life after retiring in one's sixties, whatever one has "retired" from, the pleasure I experienced beyond my job at Columbia, is a gift of life in the last decades, but it is not easily learned. As E. M. Forster so brilliantly put it, "It is difficult, after accepting six cups of tea, to throw the seventh in the face of your hostess." But sometimes, the only way to live is to get out, or at least seriously to contemplate getting out, doing the impossible, flinging the conventional tea.

Marvell's famous plea to his mistress in perhaps the best-known of the "gather ye rosebuds while ye may" poems, those elegant attempts at persuading young women to discard their virginity, argues that, in this life, we have not "world enough, and time" to dally. In an earlier work of mine, I interpreted this line to mean that those who had "world" enough, that is, those engaged in a demanding daily vocation, were short of time, while those without regular obligations had more than sufficient time, but no world. Would I, having left the "world," find myself with empty days, with time, as Virginia Woolf used to say, flapping around me? Now that I had liberated myself from a job filled with tension, now that my children had undertaken their own lives, how would I fill my time? In my sixties, I was to discover that the strict bifurcation I had earlier insisted upon between world and time was no longer applicable.

The poet May Sarton used, in some of her lower moments, to quote Richard II's sad line: "I wasted time, and now doth time waste me." She was not speaking particularly of her last years, but of those periods during which one seems to get nothing done, or nothing that offers a sense of fulfillment. The day dawns, the day passes, and there is, apart from the completion of certain necessary daily chores, nothing that leaves a glow of satisfaction. I dare say everyone has at one time or another experienced this, the sense of fragmented time, endless interruptions, and no sense of attained purpose. But after a certain age, or what we hideously call "retirement," the problem of no world, and time as a string of hours to be counted like a rosary, needs be faced. The writer Sylvia Townsend Warner, then in her sixties, wrote to a friend who was feeling the burdens of age and time:

I think as one grows older one is appallingly exposed to *wearing life* instead of living. Habit, physical deterioration and a slower digestion of our experiences, all tend to make one look on one's dear life as a garment, a dressing gown, a raincoat, a uniform, buttoned on with recurrent daily [tasks]. . . . [F]or myself I found one remedy, and that is to undertake something difficult, something new, to reroot myself in my own faculties. . . . For in such moments, life is not just a thing one wears, it is a thing one does and is.

Those of us who have retired from our "world" face the problem of what to do with time and our life, whether to wear it as a garment or to undertake "something difficult." It is not easy to decide what to undertake, what endeavor or activity will reward the devotion of one's hours in learning a new skill or acquiring new knowledge. Sadly, in our society there is a grievous need for individuals willing to dedicate their time and energies in a serious manner. There are the dying in hospices, the hungry in soup lines, the homeless in shelters, battered women and their children, the newborn abandoned to exist as "boarder babies," desperately—for their life may well depend on it—in need of company, affection, being touched or talked to. There are numerous opportunities for tutoring and teaching, projects that require patience and skill. And for those to whom "social" work does not appeal there is politics, the grassroots politics, the work in local elections, on school boards and other important bodies. There is time now to read, in a serious, organized way—all of Shakespeare, novels of a single century or country, the works of a single poet or novelist. I have a friend who at the age of sixty took up playing the piano. She will never challenge the child geniuses at Juilliard, but the satisfaction she finds is profound. Music is there to be listened to and learned about: operas, chamber music, jazz, Cole Porter. Some have always thought they might paint, or study in detail the work of a single artist or period.

The point is only that for those retired, with too much time and no world, a world must be found, and not necessarily one that is heavily populated. One can join a group or work alone; the essential, it seems to me as it did to Sylvia Townsend Warner, is that the work be difficult, concentrated, and that definite progress can be measured. If the undertaking is not to become but another daily habit, daily donned and discarded, it requires strong effort and the evidence of growing proficiency. There is, I suppose, nothing wrong with retired people taking a course here, a course there—dabbling, in short—but this defeats the purpose, which is, I believe, to maintain a carefully directed intensity.

For those who can take their world into their retirement or who do not, in any obvious sense, retire at all, the challenges are different. Here the question is one of time, and to what all that remaining time should be devoted. There are many examples of those who still have established "worlds," not in the sense of places where they receive a salary, but in the sense of what their talents have demanded of them and continue to demand.

Nora Sayre, in her book *Previous Convictions: A Journey Through the 1950s,* relates why Edmund Wilson refused to write some articles for the *New Statesman:*

explaining that he had now mapped out everything he wanted to write before the end of his life. [He was seventy-one.] He had also devised a program of reading the classics he hadn't yet ingested, and it frustrated him that he was too old to learn Chinese. He didn't speak of dying. But he said that after you'd reached a certain age, you felt the pressure of time enormously: there was so much to do, and he'd had to make a detailed schedule. (He had six years—minus a few months—left.)

Then there is Constance Garnett, who translated the great Russians into English, most of them for the first time. After the age of sixty, she continued her translations, including three plays by Turgenev when she was seventy-three; she had always regretted translating Turgenev early in her career when, she felt, she had not done him justice.

William James, for a third example, saw his last work as a completion of all that his earlier labors had led him to. He wrote at sixty-one to a friend: "I am convinced that the desire to formulate truths is a virulent disease. It has contracted an alliance lately in me with a feverish personal ambition, which I never had before, and which I recognize as an unholy thing in such a connexion. I actually dread to die until I have settled the Universe's hash in one more book."

I had thought myself, upon my retirement from Columbia, in the situation of, if not capable of the same achievements as, these three and others like them. I had always enjoyed reading biographies, finding the narrative of a life compelling, perhaps capable of suggesting as yet unanticipated adventures or possible subjects for serious perusal. I had written about biographies of women, and had, in my salad days, produced short biographies of Christopher Isherwood and the Garnetts, an English family of writers, editors, and librarians that included, by marriage, Constance Garnett. What I had not sufficiently noticed was that I was particularly drawn to the biographies of writers, of those who produced books, stories, novels, interpretations of history or literature. Even Catherine Drinker Bowen, who wrote biographies of famous lawyers and musicians, had texts or music with which to grapple.

Near the beginning of my sixties, I agreed to write the biography of Gloria Steinem. This biography of an enormously appealing person unfortunately provided me, through no fault of her own, with the wrong subject on which to devote my time in "professional" retirement, or in consideration of my personal affinities. I believe, in other words, from watching myself and others, that those of us who have been so fortunate as to take a major work of our lives into our retirements face a different danger from those whose lives must undergo more radical changes. We who continue that major work into our retirements face the danger, as I did, of undertaking the wrong task.

The five years I spent on the biography of Gloria Steinem seem to me now to have made too little use of all I had learned before, and contributed too little to what I had hoped to accomplish before death. Benefits did accrue to me, in meeting people, and to others, in learning more about Steinem in a serious and non-sensational way. Nonetheless, I consider my impulsive decision to write Steinem's biography to have been an invitation to time to waste me. In fairness, I should add that I am by no means certain of what other task might have better occupied me during those five years, but that is part of the ransom for wasted time: opportunities to discover those works that might round out a life's endeavor are wasted also.

All this was in no way Steinem's fault; the mistake was all my own. The sense I had of not having used all my talents was in no way related to Steinem herself. I do not feel in any way ashamed of the book that I finally produced, nor have I the slightest wish to repudiate it. I never doubted the importance of recording the life of a person so completely focused on the lamentable dissimilarities of opportunity that race, class, gender, and national origin enforce and reinforce in our culture. At a time when the division between the haves and the have-nots in our society expands daily, when there has never in this country been so great a gulf between the rich and the poor, the portrait of a woman devoted to alleviating these and other disparities serves, I believe, an estimable purpose; and that that woman has been, at the same time, able to explore and experience a full, if unconventional, female life adds to my sense of accomplishment in having written this biography.

Why then do I have a sense of time ill spent? In all the other occasions, events, and undertakings of my sixties, whether a house, a dog, or the contemplation of death, I emerged somehow changed, refigured, with my life altered to extend the range of possible reactions and experiences, however subtle or internal. The meanings of much that had puzzled me in life became clearer, seemed suddenly to find their place in a long history of disparate emotions and perceptions. None of this occurred in the writing of Steinem's biography. Certainly, I learned a lot. As I reported in the book, Steinem spent twenty years during which there was only one week when she wasn't in an airplane on a mission of support for a cause. In following her travels, I discovered much about the founding of shelters, women-run businesses, Native American achievements, African American accomplishments, and more.

There is a price for everything in life; as Lionel Trilling used to put it, we pay for our experiences with more than equal coin. And to become the public, generous, productive person, able to work effectively for the righting of many social wrongs, Steinem required a personality ill at ease with introspection, or indeed any deep sense of a self in conflict with her mission. She turned to introspection in any degree only when she was well past fifty and desperately weary, and while that belated experience of introspection has allowed her to live in more comfortable domestic circumstances and to spend more time writing, it has not, in any essential way, altered her remarkable fitness for the external, public life she has always pursued. Thus Steinem, for me, was a biographical subject lacking a subtext. How confounding it was that I, who had urged women to delve deeply beneath the surface, found myself with a subject who had little interest in delving. Still, my hope for the biography had been to allow women to discover, using Steinem's life as a model, the possibility of avoiding conventional gender expectations, or at least of not adopting them unthinkingly. Perhaps it has had that effect, here or there.

For myself, the sensation of learning was intermittent at best, and it was more a sensation of accumulation than learning. I now suspect that, as a solitary individual without a wide and varied circle of friends, I had hoped to encounter some people who might expand the range of my companionships. Alas, this did not happen. After the book's completion, it was as though the whole experience had disappeared forever, fading back into the remembered five years and leaving not a trace behind. Traces, I now believe, are left only by work that has overmastered us, work which we cannot, after we once begin it, imagine not in our life.

And this is very odd in a way. For whom did I meet or find companionship with by buying a small house or acquiring a dog? Other dog walkers, met casually in the park, with whom there was no conversation but pleasant exchanges that were warming; men who mowed lawns and plowed driveways, whose way of life was harsh, dependent on the weather and the incredible infidelity of machinery. Why did these, with whom I talked of nothing in the slightest degree significant, seem to move me to new capacities in my sixties? Why did my daily life, my conversations with friends and my children, seem to move me toward wisdom or new insights when those five years of biography writing did not? Perhaps biography by its very nature induces such a reaction. I was amused to learn from a member of a biography seminar to which I used to belong that the title of a recent session was "Why I Will Never Write Another Biography." The reasons given included: It's thankless, demeaning, doesn't pay, ruins your health, ruins your bank account, there's no truth, etc. Biography itself, it would appear, can be a trap.

There may even be harsher aspects to my decision to undertake that biography. Was I caught up in a kind of media-hype excitement, beguiled by a celebrity world I had never cared for, from which I falsely expected some new experience, perhaps even some new thrills? Because Steinem is a feminist and a worker for social change, was I the more able to disguise this unsuitable attraction under persuasive guises? Had I failed to see that if one's sixties are to be devoted to a particular task, that task must be in keeping with the tone and substance of one's previous work?

It is possible that I undertook the task out of a kind of loneliness I thought this enterprise would counter. If that was my hope, I was wrong. One is either a solitary or not. And solitaries, who work and think alone, are quite unlikely to be plucked from that condition by a leap into the company (and contemplation) of a busy, socially committed person. Steinem, who lives alone, is not a solitary. I, who do not live alone and have lived with three children and a husband, am. I have, in fact, as the only child of relaxed, remarkably unanxious and detached parents, always lived with a certain degree of solitude.

With solitude, of course, however fervently it is desired and embraced, comes loneliness. Alfred Kazin, at eighty, publishing excerpts from his lifelong journal, ended his book with a quotation from Henry James: "The starting point of my life has been loneliness." Loneliness is probably the finishing point too, but I suspect now that I may have hoped to find an antidote to loneliness in the writing of Steinem's life, and this was an expectation on my part in no way practical or wise.

Sylvia Townsend Warner, whose words in all cases, including her advice to her friend, I found both wise and elegant, had herself undertaken at the age of seventy the biography of a man she had never met, although he had acclaimed her and once written to her in praise of her work. He was T. H. White, the author of *The Once and Future King* (a book transformed into the musical *Camelot*), a lonely man, devoted to animals, whose advice to those in sadness was not unlike Sylvia Townsend Warner's to those burdened with meaningless time: the only cure for sadness, White said, was to learn something. Clearly, Townsend Warner had long admired White and felt a kinship with him before being asked, shortly after his death, to write his biography. "The essential in a biography, so I believe," she explained to a correspondent at the conclusion of her task, "is that the subject of the biography should have known himself, and that T. H.

White certainly did." This sentence struck home to me, because Steinem had not known herself, not in the sense of acting from hidden, unadmitted motives—this she never did—but in the sense of not having needed, for her own survival, to penetrate her own psyche.

Warner's reasons for undertaking her biography ironically echoed my own reasons for undertaking the Steinem biography: "One has a dozen motives, hasn't one? I did partly undertake it as a dare; seventy is rather an advanced age to begin an entirely different technique. Partly as a rescue operation [the alternative biographer was considered incompetent by White's literary executors and friends]. . . . Partly because I wanted to do something that would take a long time and involve some sort of research." Also, she knew from the first day she visited White's home, in which he had died four months before, that writing his biography was "a human obligation." I think I felt all of those motives. But mine would not be, as Townsend Warner's was, the last biography of its subject. And the writer of literary texts, like T. H. White, is easier to interpret, if one is oneself a writer and critic, than the effective doer of deeds of support and kindness.

My life following those years took on more spirit and more chances to write. Just as Käthe Kollwitz had spoken of a rising tide, so Sylvia Townsend Warner wrote in her diary at sixty-nine: "I woke up *knowing* that I wanted to write and knowing what I wanted to write about. It is odd that after this long and agonizing interim of fret and complete drought, I scarcely even feel relieved. I just feel confident and forward-going. And I have not the slightest notion what set me going again. I was not. Suddenly, I am."

Sylvia Townsend Warner is witness to the delight one may savor in one's mid-sixties. "In the evening," she recorded in her diary, "the Amadeus [Quartet] played opus 132; and I danced to the last movement, I rose up & danced, among the cats, & their saucers, and only when I was too far carried away to stop did I realize that I was behaving very oddly for my age—and that perhaps it was the last time I would dance for joy."

The greatest oddity of one's sixties is that, if one dances for joy, one always supposes it is for the last time. Yet this supposition provides the rarest and most exquisite flavor to one's later years. The piercing sense of "last time" adds intensity, while the possibility of "again" is never quite effaced.

E-MAIL

Cecily: And this is the box in which I keep all your dear letters.

Algernon: My letters! But, my own sweet Cecily, I have never written you any letters

Cecily: You need hardly remind me of that. I remember only too well that I was forced to write your letters for you.

—OSCAR WILDE, *The Importance of Being Earnest*

AGING, particularly in the later decades, is a drawing-in. Encounters with the outside world diminish for many reasons, not all of them to do with fear, negligence, or lack of energy. The solitude of old age is often pleasurable, offering, I sometimes think, a pleasure similar to those described by converts to a religion. There is peace, a sense of the present—if one has been awakened to new possibilities—rather than the past or the future, a looking within to discover, as many religions urge us to do, inner wisdom. But conversion, either religious or personal, is not universal in old age: loneliness and a sense of meaninglessness to one's life in contrast to the life in the work world, the whirring world, are far more common. Many of us can, at various harried times in our life, feel alone and assaulted by the meaninglessness of what we are doing. But, at such times, we *are* doing; the problem is not a lack of activity with a point, but rather questions about the point of the activity. These later malaises are not only ordinary but difficult to parry or to change. The world outside neither cares nor offers attentiveness, except occasionally. If one ventures out to meet others like oneself, the conversation is predictable, the discussions repetitive; shared hopelessness may rescue one from the sense of a uniquely empty destiny, but it hardly comforts.

Which brings me to e-mail. Conversing via computer may not be a problem in the years to come when most people will use computers and will be accustomed to reaching into the world "out there" through the Internet and especially through e-mail. One of the educational hopes of those running this country, or trying to, is that each twelve-year-old will be enabled to enter the Internet. This is, I am certain, a fine aim, but for the present I would rather begin a campaign urging every person without an ongoing compulsion in her life to learn to use a computer at least well enough to dip into e-mail. In an even more revolutionary mode, I would endeavor to put a personal computer in every retirement home, apartment, or dwelling, privately or centrally operated. E-mail is the perfect way to encounter the world outside one's own private domain without filling out any forms, enrolling, traveling, or revealing anything whatsoever about oneself unless choosing to do so.

Let us take families, for a start. Sure, if we have a family, it will try to visit and to keep in touch, but how often? And with what enthusiasm? Yet with e-mail an older person can keep in touch with everyone, can encourage (I know cases where this has worked wonderfully well) round robin letters in which each family member adds his or her bit and sends it on. Old enmities and grudges need not stand in the way of this. I am reminded of a situation where a grandmother did not especially like the woman a male relative of hers had married, and she found herself sadly out of touch with the man because his wife had actively discouraged social contact. But his uxorial loyalties did not extend to e-mail. My friend and her male relative exchange frequent e-mail messages and accounts of their lives, and who's to know? Similarly, old friends will "get in touch" by this means, providing (and there is always ample protection from intrusion) the chance of "catching up" with people unlikely to be encountered in any other way.

Above all, it is the instantaneous quality of e-mail that is so appealing and, in our world, unique. One need not telephone and catch people unready for conversation or, far more likely these days, leave a message whose receipt is hardly certain. One need not search for a pen, postage stamp, or mailbox, or depend on the ever-more-uncertain post office, whose precarious and delayed deliveries have become known to users of e-mail as "snail mail." One simply sits down, boots up the machine, calls up the e-mail dispenser, and shoots off a message that, with its immediacy and lack of deliberation, is probably more direct than anything written by other means, and therefore very likely to inspire a similar response.

I have never been a stranger to computers for the purposes of writing. Word processing, as it was called from the first, was, like the typewriter that preceded it, my instrument of choice. From a very early age I had learned to touch-type. My father insisted that I must type fast, even over my protests that I never wanted to be a secretary or typist. Despite my protests, that is of course exactly what I became in my first job at a publishing firm, a job that I, like every other book-loving college graduate from that day to this, had sought. One of the results of this, not unnaturally, was that I did a lot of typing for my husband—although, to be fair, he did a great many other editorial tasks for me. When I finally bought him a computer a few years back, in time for his third book, I had managed to convince him that one-finger typing was more common than not, especially among men, and overnight he became a devotee of the monitor and keyboard. He, however, has not yet succumbed to e-mail, being quite able to shout to me from his neighboring study and insisting that anyone else can telephone. I'm working on it.

But I, no more than he, rarely ventured beyond word processing. That was how I wrote, and writing was what I mainly did. As something called the Internet, and eventually the World Wide Web, began to intrude upon my consciousness, I ignored it as assiduously as did most people of my age or older, convinced that this was a future phenomenon with which, given the shortness of our time and the limits of our scope, we could comfortably have nothing to do.

Then e-mail entered my life. It turned out that despite having retired from Columbia, I was still entitled to use its facilities. At the price of two twelve-foot lengths of telephone wire, to reach from the computer to my phone box, and two little gadgets to connect the wires to each other, I could be on e-mail. Columbia gave me a disk that let me into the system, and voilà!

Voilà? I had no idea what to do next; I knew, in fact, nothing of moving beyond the contents of my own computer. Then a friend of mine, an intimate since graduate school (and of him more later) came, as he has for all the twenty years I have had a computer, to my aid. Frank set it all up, leaving my head whirling with complicated directions that turned out to be, of course, simplicity itself once mastered, and sent me off to Columbia where, in person, I had to acquire a password. The cost of e-mail, I gratefully learned, was the cost of a phone call from my apartment to Columbia, thirty blocks away; with e-mail I could reach, for the same price, anyone similarly equipped, anywhere in the world.

I was still dubious. There was the telephone, the

fax machine. Most important, I am that rapidly disappearing creature, a writer of letters. What further means of communication did I require? It turned out that I required e-mail to give me back almost daily, continuing communication with another dear friend from graduate school, who lived in the Midwest and was stubbornly incapable of writing: letters, academic papers, books, or, so he insisted, anything. He did write on student papers, for he is a professor and one of the best teachers in the country, a claim I can make without fear of contradiction. Teaching, together with exchanges with students, is his passion, and fortunately his university, in a time wiser in some ways than now, gave him tenure without publications; he had somehow struggled through the completion of a (written) Ph.D.

Jonathan and I talked on the phone with some fortnightly regularity, and I found these conversations to be all that dialogue between friends can aspire to; but these exchanges were intermittent and, inevitably, some topics we could each have benefited from discussing dropped into the interstices of life between calls. And then Jon, presented by his university with a desktop computer, found himself capable of e-mail. Each of us called up our e-mail once a day, and we could respond, spontaneously and without undue preparation, to what the other had written. This exchange, though not simultaneous, allowed for spontaneity and the immediacy of speech. One does not, as in a letter however rapidly composed, stop to consider what one will say. Certainly spelling errors and typos pass unnoticed; sentence structure is frequently lost in the outpouring of observations and responses. Not to mention that if one suddenly thinks of something one is impelled to communicate, one can leave a missive on e-mail before one forgets the matter, knowing it will, within no more than a day, reach its object and be noted.

I know of those who carry on distant love affairs with far more satisfaction—and more extended arguments and discussions—than the telephone would allow or they could afford. Information, similarly though less fervently, is easily obtainable, or at least easily requested. All the respondent need do is hit the reply key or click the mouse on the reply icon, and answer the question. Bliss. And suppose that one has decided in one's later years to take up some subject or course of study or frivolous passion: no matter what it is, there will be others throughout the world to communicate with about it. The danger is, of course, that one will be overwhelmed with hundreds of replies, but those threatened with isolation and the same daily intercourse may want to choose among the respondents and plunge further into dialogue. Or not. I know someone who asked on the Internet if anyone was interested in a certain painter: he received two hundred responses. It was not exactly a minor painter, but the response did suggest to me, when an old woman in Florida complained of the fact that she discusses nothing but cottage cheese and everyone's children each day, that she might do well to pick a slightly more daring subject and plunge in. Not only does one not have to be a rocket scientist to work a computer and venture into the beyond, but one can be the most simple-minded person alive, used to only old, familiar ways. Rapport can follow or expand. Even if one does not, as I do, know a Jonathan, one can tap the computer in search of someone with a passion similar to one's own.

Jonathan and I respond easily and quickly to each other by e-mail, often writing more than we meant to write, saying more than we meant to say. Thus have I acquired, through a scorned medium, a closeness that for years I have not felt to this dear friend. Many others reach me on e-mail, but most of them are people I see regularly, or who are getting in touch infrequently from distant parts. These can sometimes be long exchanges, helpful and comforting. But with e-mail, Jonathan and I have conquered a distance that we traveled in person only once every two or three years.

We met in graduate school, although he is five years younger than I; we were at different stages. Our first serious conversations began when he wheeled his two babies, and I my three, up and down in Riverside Park, speaking of literature. I can recall our coming to the end of a path and, without comment, turning the carriages and starting back the other way, still talking.

Perhaps because women were scarce on the ground when I was in graduate school and determined to become a professional woman, I have preserved from that time friendships with two men who have, as Browning put it, grown "old along with me." I think these friendships have endured for over forty years because these men have, as I like to think I have, changed with the world and not taken refuge in "better" or "more traditional" times. Each of these men understands my feminism, and the problems faced by women in our society. They have become devoid of macho qualities, and are encouraging of their wives' changing expectations.

Jon not only loves teaching, he is the only professor I have ever known who relishes the classroom and is not happy away from it; while the rest of us long for leaves, he will write to me on e-mail that there are only two weeks left until the summer term, in which he always voluntarily teaches, begins. Jon is a Hebrew scholar and attended a yeshiva; asked once at dinner by someone if he would ever today consider becoming an observant Jew, he answered that he would think about it when he finished his pork chop. Utterly kind, utterly candid, he is, oddly—or perhaps because we meet so seldom and talk only by telephone and e-mail—the single one of my two male friends with whom I discuss sex in some detail. This arises more from his experiences than mine, but there is nothing, with our computer voices, that we feel we cannot speak of.

My other friend from graduate school, Frank, is my age and, among all his other talents and attributes, is a computer buff. Without him, I could scarcely have moved from my incredibly expensive first computer to my latest one (electronic equipment is the only aspect of modern life that has notably come to cost less and less with the years) and it was he who set me up on e-mail. Unlike today's doctors, Frank, though a busy man, will pay house calls to rescue me from the muddles into which I plunge with sad regularity. He and I communicate by e-mail on matters of meetings and politics as well as personal messages, but because of my computer muddles I see him a few times more than I might otherwise. (Everyone with a computer, needs, honesty forces me to confess, a computer buff acquaintance who will rally round when needed. Oddly enough, this is not hard to find among the younger generation of whom many live for computers and actually enjoy coping with them even in aid of relative ignoramuses.)

Frank has, in recent years, become devoted to Haiti, visiting there often. This dedication induces in me a certain guilt for my limited political focus on women, but when he e-mails to me letters on Haiti and asks me to send them on, I do so. E-mail, therefore, has made me more a part of his life than I might otherwise be, and allows me to feel politically active: a good feeling. It was, I now recognize, his belief that I could benefit from transformation to e-mail that has enriched my life politically as well as personally.

I think there is almost nothing each of us could ask of the other in vain, and though we do not discuss our thoughts by e-mail, as I do with Jon, it might well be by e-mail that we would find each other in need. E-mail is not only a habit that can be depended on by senders and receivers, it is also very much a one-on-one form of communication. Telephones ring; voices can be overheard, but with e-mail, one moves into it without notice, and may find there messages that are not, strangely enough, appropriate for the telephone.

I am fortunate in having come to computer use and e-mail before my last decades. But that need not, should not, must not deter anyone. There are people out there ready to talk to anybody about anything— and this is not meant to be a sweeping statement or an exaggeration. One can speak to family, friends, strangers, or half-remembered acquaintances. Reaching out into the world, one gets a sharp thrill, a new sensation to spark one's daily life, satisfactory or not. If one sometimes feels compelled, as we all do, to complain about any dimension or all dimensions of one's life but does not do so because all the people one sees are sick of it and will visit even less often if complaints or criticisms are forced upon them, well, there are people out there who will be happy to exchange complaints and perhaps even help to talk us out of them, or counter them with other, strange grievances.

As I say: I'd like to put a functioning computer tied to the Internet and e-mail in the home of everyone over sixty-five. Especially in the homes of those who think computers belong only to the future, of which they are not a part, or who think because they cannot program their VCR they cannot operate e-mail.

I hope it is now obvious that e-mail is especially suited, as I have found, to those of us no longer revolving our days around the working world. It reaches into our privacy without invading it, an astonishing accomplishment; it connects us to those with whom the possibility of connection might have remained unexpected; it offers us welcome without the necessity for social arrangements; it inspires us to confidences and the practice of wit.

And, unlike Cecily, we do not need to hope in vain for correspondents, or write the letters we might so bleakly have wanted to receive. It is a liberating thought.

A UNIQUE PERSON

She knew enough of the world to see how badly people longed to be known and how they suffered when they were not, how a small fame fed the hunger for a larger, and how painful and corrosive both hunger and fame could be.

—ROBERT MEZEY, writing about Virginia Hamilton Adair

MAY SARTON lived as an anomaly and has remained one after her death in 1995, at the age of eighty-three. I met her at the beginning of her sixties, when she had recently moved to a lonely house in the small town of Nelson, New Hampshire; she died at the end of my sixties. Throughout the intervening years she bravely lived the inevitable contradictions of her chosen life, wailing her complaints the while. She had determined to live a life outside of urban communities of writers and the fellowship that flourishes in cities; she wished for solitude and yet yearned to be recognized by those she considered "respected critics"—it was a phrase often on her lips. She bitterly resented the attention assiduously paid by the eastern establishment to writers less productive and less read than she, yet she knew herself not suited to the frantic social life so much a part of that literary world. Indeed, she was unwilling even to enter the social life, such as it was, of Nelson.

If I accepted invitations I would soon be giving invitations myself, and the whole atmosphere of the house would be subtly changed. I was surprised to discover how strongly I felt about *not* having cocktail parties here.

Indeed, after years of gregariousness, of meeting famous people, she now recognized that if she was to make her mark as a writer and poet she needed a regular daily schedule, a life without the daily domestic demands of others, and—essential always for May Sarton—a garden.

I was reminded of her recently when *The New Yorker,* a magazine for which she once wrote, but which, together with the rest of the literary establishment, ignored her in later years, published a picture of "literary lions" at the New York Public Library. How Sarton would have liked to have been there, or at similar events, such as the annual meeting of the American Academy of Arts and Letters, which had scorned her. Yet, looking at that photograph, which included such figures as Henry Kissinger, Betty Friedan, and Gay Talese, I knew that were Sarton still alive, while she would be envious of their recognition and publicity, she would also be contemptuous of the Library's idea of literary lions: this conflict was sharp and continuous. Most ironically, there was probably no one in that photograph who had thirty-eight books currently in print—that is, selling, and worth keeping on the shelves in bookstores.

Many writers fall between two stools: Sarton fell between stools past counting. In today's publishing world, for example, where the great majority of editors are very young, and only a few battle-worn warriors endure, Sarton is largely an unfamiliar name. A casual poll of my own in these precincts revealed ignorance of her and her works. Sarton has long been published by one of the few remaining independent and long-established publishing companies—W. W. Norton—and they have for years simply printed whatever she gave them—poetry, journals, novels, memoirs—in the happy assurance that it would sell. For many years she had one wonderfully supportive editor there, a man elegant in his manner who treated her with a gallantry to which she always happily responded, but his whole-hearted support came at the price of the careful editing she very much needed but did not want. As I look back now, it is clear that her editor and publisher should have pushed harder. True, she did not take criticism well, and was averse to, indeed downright stubborn about, rewriting. Still, some careful editing might have made a difference in the reception of her books by the literary and reviewing establishment, many of whom lost the benefit of her ideas and insights, so I believe, because they stumbled over repeated metaphors and lazy comparisons. She once mentioned that a man's eye twinkled many times in the first chapter of a novel, but berated me when I mentioned it. I never quite stopped mentioning these things, however ineffectually, and that may be, among other reasons, why she trusted me.

Not all the young, of course, look blank upon the mention of the name May Sarton. Some younger academics have recently been writing critically about her work, and several volumes of such criticism have emerged in the last few years from university presses. The fact about Sarton, who had long been literally deluged with loving letters from her readers while being treated with disdain or indifference by reviewers, is that readers find her as individuals, read her as individuals, and continue thereafter to read everything she published. She offers to those, particularly women, whose lives are not defined only by the sophisticated eastern seaboard's literary insiders, a sense of their inherent value, a promise of their chance for change, and the discovery that someone understands and can convey the courage and gallantry of their existence. They have always been able, furthermore, to see that her writing is art, not pap, or how-to instructions, or easy consolation: by writing of her own life, she illuminates theirs.

Yet she often counted her life a failure because she was not a literary lion, not a member of the dinnerparty circle of New York writers, not one whom the marketing forces behind literary events noticed. She continued to mourn the fact that so few of her admirers were famous in the *New Yorker* mode, never recognizing that she had outgrown that mode and contributed to a genre of literature far braver and far more innovative. Men as well as women acknowledged the value of her unique voice; it was a man who organized a conference to celebrate her eightieth year.

Some of the acclaim she had longed for came in her old age, but not, even then, in the form she wanted it. I knew of her longing to be in the Academy of Arts and Letters, and when Jacques Barzun was head of that organization, and still a friend of mine, I approached him without her knowledge asking if she might be chosen. He replied that, having inquired, he had been told she was only a "woman's writer." That, of course, was long ago, probably in the early seventies. In later years, she even managed occasionally to find humor in the series of dreadful reviews she had had in *The New York Times Book Review* for more than seventeen years. Better reviews came at last in her eighties, but she never ceased, despite the humor, to bristle at the memory of the bad ones.

That Sarton was one of the earliest lesbians to "come out"—a phrase she loathed—had endeared her to other lesbians less inclined to so naming themselves at that early a date. More recently, in our franker time, lesbians have acclaimed her as a foremother—an expression that always reminded her of foreplay, and one she equally detested. Sarton wrote of aging before that became a marketable subject, and of solitude when the solitary seemed at best objects of compassion. She had many muses, many loves, many, many devoted readers, but these were never enough.

Of the four genres in which Sarton worked—poetry, journals, memoirs, novels—the novels were the weakest. This was the area in which she most required the discipline of the revision and compression for which she would never sit still. It is true that not all editing is benign or even helpful; the talents of a good editor who still preserves the voice of the writer have always been rare, never less so than today. In this connection, I have often amused myself by picturing Virginia Woolf in the hands of one of today's unseasoned editors—who, even if not young, are, by necessity, more often concerned with marketing than with the finer points of literature. "But Mrs. Woolf, you can't possibly expect to sell a novel with a heroine past fifty." "Mrs. Woolf, who on earth is going to read a novel in which you can't tell who's talking to whom and when?" "Mrs. Woolf, do you think it's convincing to portray your heroine as two hundred and fifty years old?" And so forth. Woolf was a genius as well as a compulsive reviser, and thrived on the fact that she was her own publisher and need not heed any editor's fears and emendations. But Sarton could have used editing and did not get it.

Yet when she got it right, it was amazingly right, and she got it right more often than not. My reading of her 1968 memoir, *Plant Dreaming Deep,* a work that quite literally caught me in its spell, was the beginning of our friendship. Rereading that book today, I still encounter what excited me; I still hear her voice speaking to me of life's possibilities. "We have to make myths of our lives," she wrote. "It is the only way to live without despair." As she reached the end of her account of buying the house in Nelson and establishing herself there, she reported: "When I first arrived, everything was an adventure, and it is that adventure that this book recounts. But already that exuberance, that time when I was in a perpetual state of wonder, curiosity, and sometimes dismay and fear, is changing. The romantic period of my life here is coming to a close." Was it reading her observation "It is only past the meridian of fifty that one can believe that the universal sentence of death applies to oneself" that prepared me for what would become my fascination with the liminal experience of fifty? Sarton's wisdom was, for me as for many, a support and a promise offered by someone who had been there before and could explain the journey.

Maxine Kumin has written in another connection, "Ours is the friendship that never happened, that cannot end." That phrase neatly evokes my relation to Sarton, who taught me that a life devoted to solitude is also often a life constantly bedeviled by rage. She welcomed me, in 1972, as a critic, an academic, a scholar, but could never forgive me for not being an unmodified admirer. She was, certainly from the time I first knew her, deluged with adorers, fans, visitors and letter-writers in love with her life, fulsome with praise. They never satisfied her, not being established critics, yet she was furious with me because there were a few critical remarks (about her metaphors) in my largely adulatory 1974 preface to a reissue of her novel *Mrs. Stevens Hears the Mermaids Singing*. I had written it in the hope of introducing her to the academic community, but she screamed at me for its failure to celebrate her effort with undiluted appreciation. At the same time, however, because I never became an acolyte, I earned a place in her life that might have been otherwise unoccupied. I think this is why she early made me her literary executor and did not change her mind despite her many angry words against me. She welcomed, I suspect, the distance I offered, freedom, despite her rages, from the intensity of her many passions. Her lovers were her muses—often, it seemed to me, in reverse proportion to their malleability. I was not, and would never be, in love with her, nor she with me. I was the stuff of which literary executors, not muses, are made.

When I met her, however, when I wrote to her and sent her some of my articles, I was in love with what I thought I saw in *Plant Dreaming Deep:* an account of how solitude can be shown to be a possible life for women. I was, in 1972, a professor, the mother of three teenage children, the wife of a professor, the daughter of parents with whom I was, happily, in constant touch, and a writer engrossed, at that time, with the idea of androgyny. The thought of solitude tempted me, certainly as she presented it, with Faustian force. Not only had Sarton chosen to live alone, Sarton had planned the house she would occupy, had seen that it was fixed up as a nest, a workplace, truly a home of one's own. The furniture inherited from her parents was moved in; she was surrounded only by what she wished to see. In addition, she had the sense of a guardian angel as having found the house for her and offered her, at just the right time, those individuals who might help her to achieve her dream, to make it a reality—guardian angels in the form of infrequently met friends and advisers. However dubious of religion, she had always a sense of hints, of guidance, of messages coming at exactly the right moment, and I recognized the experience. As Sartre brilliantly suggested, we moderns may not believe in the Father or the Son, but we understand the Holy Ghost.

With a life full of palpable fulfillment and possibility, I longed for solitude in a place of my own with a passion that has not abated, although it has, in a manner of speaking, been satisfied. The solitude Sarton represented might have driven me into mad rages, as it did her; the solitude I found in my sixties, with ample private space but with steady companionship, was what I did not then know I wanted. Sarton herself came to realize that she had failed to express her anger in *Plant Dreaming Deep*. But at the time I read it, I was beguiled, bewitched. I wrote to her and we met.

I can remember every moment of that visit, and of subsequent ones, before our friendship became almost entirely enacted on the telephone; but that first visit is most clearly recalled. I spent the night at a motel nearby, or what passed for nearby in rural New Hampshire, and drove over the following morning to meet her at her house in Nelson. Snow was on the ground, and she was standing outside to greet me. I'm very bad on noticing clothes, let alone remembering them, but I seem to see her in a sheepskin jacket. She took me off immediately to see her small-town neighborhood. At a nearby farm I was introduced to Esmeralda, the donkey she had borrowed for a time as a kind of therapy, and later written about in a delightful book, *The Poet and the Donkey*. (In that book she turned herself into an aging male poet, the better to deal with his/her fascination with a woman college administrator, an obsession Sarton was undergoing at the time.) Esmeralda welcomed the peppermints we had brought; I met the Shetland sheepdog puppies, one of whom would become her much-loved Tamas; and all the while we talked, getting to know each other. Returning to the house, I admired it, how each of its rooms served her purposes and resonated to her elegant versions of beauty—the painted floors, the delicate arrangements of flowers everywhere, even in winter (for she would always buy flowers even with half the money she had left for food), the sense of space and light, the atmosphere of a home devoted above all else to work. That night she screamed at me for the first time; I had dipped her ivory-handled knives into the dishwater.

She broke unexpectedly and often, as I soon

learned, into rages, and I was later to discover from her journal that because I had told her I thought she was a genius, a discoverer of woman's solitude, she cried in bed that night. She was to scream at me in rage many times more, at first in person, later on the telephone; but after nearly leaving her house in fury once at her attacks, I learned to recognize them as the necessary outbursts for which friends must serve when there is no live-in companion.

By the time I turned sixty, Sarton had become a steady figure in my mental landscape, although I saw her rarely after that. It was in my sixty-first year (and her seventy-fifth) that I gave her Pierrot. Sarton had once told me that she wanted her next cat to be a Himalayan—one of those facts I tucked away. In 1986 Sarton's much-loved cat Bramble died. Tamas, Sarton's sweet Shetland sheepdog was getting old and fragile. I had visions of Sarton bereft of Tamas and with no other animal to comfort her, a crisis to be avoided at all costs. So I began to search for a Himalayan kitten, which is to say that I consulted my daughter Margaret, who is the most efficient person I know at tracking anything down. She was not encouraging; her first searches revealed that Himalayan cats were mostly bred in some midwestern state, I forget which, and one would have to be shipped by air to its new home. I felt I wanted to see the kitten before giving it to Sarton; I couldn't have it shipped to me since our own cat, Toby, was not given to feline welcomings. And so, for a short time, the matter rested.

But Margaret, once on a trail, does not give up. She read the classified ads and discovered one for pure-bred Himalayan kittens, telephone number provided. I called and learned that these Himalayan kittens had been born some weeks before at the house of a couple who lived just around the corner from me. (Sarton's guardian angel was still hovering.) Margaret and I made an appointment to visit. It had to be an absolutely enchanting kitten, I told Margaret; I was not allowed to be my usual gushing self with animals.

There were six kittens, all males. Sarton had wanted a female, but not unequivocally. It is unusual for a litter to be all one sex; these looked so alike we hardly knew which to choose, nor have I any way of knowing if we got the one we picked. The owners kindly agreed, if we bought the kitten, to keep it until we could take it directly to Sarton on the weekend. What tipped the scale was the mother cat's name: Miss Cecily Cardew. All that family's pets were named after characters in Oscar Wilde's *The Importance of Being Earnest;* their Scottie was named Gwendolen. Margaret had been a magnificent Lady Bracknell in a school performance: obviously, the die was cast. We had bought a cream-colored Himalayan kitten with an impressive pedigree.

The airlines were unwilling to take the kitten without extensive notice, and other animal reservations preceded mine. I decided therefore to drive the kitten to the Boston airport, where I would leave the rented car and be met by Nancy Hartley, Sarton's secretary.

Margaret agreed to come along to keep me company and to try to soothe the kitten, snatched from his home, his mother and his brothers, and rudely thrust into a continuously vibrating vehicle. Margaret did her best, but the kitten was not easily soothed; he lay in her lap, panting, with his tongue out. By the time I gave up the rented car at the airport, saw Margaret off to visit friends in Boston, and moved myself and the kitten to Nancy Hartley's car, the kitten had decided I was the enemy. He spent the drive to Maine (May had recently moved from Nelson to York, Maine) in Nancy's lap, hunched below the steering wheel, and refused, from the moment we arrived (and through all my subsequent visits), to have anything to do with me. I had a large scotch, while Sarton looked troubled, not without reason.

The kitten, once in the house, refused to be caught, and when caught, escaped, always to a more inaccessible place. Sarton was distraught. Tamas was wary. I was exhausted. Eventually, we all retired for the night, the kitten in Sarton's room. With only a wall separating us, I heard Sarton in the morning complaining to someone on the telephone about the kitten. "He's so young, and I'm so old," she cried, "and I just can't cope with all this." It was hardly a marvelous beginning; I was downhearted; the truth is, I reminded myself, that most efforts made on Sarton's behalf take a while to become appreciated. When Nancy drove me to the airport for my flight home, I said to her: "If she decides against the kitten, please

find a home for him here. I can't come back for him."
Nancy, ever reassuring, reassured me. The next I heard
the kitten had been named Pierrot, and was flourishing. He was almost white, although he darkened
somewhat with time, and his points were blue. Sarton
feared, with good reason, that a hawk, seeing him
agleam in the moonlight, might snatch him, as a hawk
had snatched Doris Lessing's full-grown cat in Africa
long ago. But Pierrot endured; he prevailed, outlasting
a wirehaired dachshund puppy who *was* too much for
Sarton, and, at last, poor, much-missed Tamas. He
grew to be a very large, monumental cat, gazing about
Buddha-like, with nothing to fear from hawks or anyone else and ruling Sarton with kingly assurance.
When I visited Sarton in the years after his arrival, he
snubbed me pointedly. No matter: Pierrot remains the
most satisfactory present (as well as the most expensive, Himalayan kittens, rented cars, and air tickets
costing what they do) that I have ever given anyone.

In the years that followed, our few meetings were
not ideal. Sarton always longed for company and then
resented the company for keeping her from her work,
for requiring attention, probably even a meal. Guests
were always sincerely encouraged to visit, then always
on the day secretly unwelcome. I almost never stay
overnight with anyone, even family, but with Sarton,
after the long drive to reach her in her isolated house
by the sea in Maine, there was no choice. In the morning, we parted with great affection and relief. We
wrote few letters; most of those were about some

problem or other, or mere notes. The telephone became the instrument of our friendship, the device that made our relationship possible and helped me to keep a running account of her life over the years.

Her place in my life was simply in being May Sarton. I was there to hear her news, to absorb her bitterness and anger, which she knew I would not repeat, to respond, if possible, with comfort and laughter. As she aged, she feared her solitude might turn to loneliness, because, as she wrote in *After the Stroke,* she had lost her "self." I went to see her in the late 1970s after her stroke, and found her quite vigorous; rather to my dismay, she drove me to the bus that would return me to my summer home. She recovered her "self," and with it her range of complaints, but she had, as she knew, taken "a leap into old age."

One of the rewards of this leap was her renewed correspondence with Juliette Huxley, whom she had loved for many years, and who reached out to Sarton in old age across an abyss of hurt silence. (Juliette had cut off all communication after her belated discovery of Sarton's affair with Juliette's husband, Julian Huxley, a famous scientist and the brother of Aldous.) Sarton had at first been seduced by Julian and, indeed, entranced by him, but had soon transferred her passion to Juliette. And Sarton would later admit that the only letters she really enjoyed writing or receiving were to or from Juliette; Sarton had in fact at the time of her death collected her many letters to Juliette with the thought of possible publication. At the same time, she could not give up the compulsion to answer the enormous number of letters that reached her daily from those she had never met, or knew but slightly, and her ultimate inability to do so haunted her to the end.

In the journal of her eighty-second year, published posthumously, she would say, "The wish to die is staggering." In those last years, she mentioned that wish but never believed it was right to consider taking one's life. By the end, I too wished for her death; she was so miserable, unable to perform even the simplest household chores without extreme fatigue, above all, unable to write or even to compose poems in her head. I believe her doctors thought hers were problems of old age and couldn't be helped, and she was grateful for their opinions. They quite clearly believed her life was ending, and that there was nothing to be done. She was afflicted with so many ailments—strokes, cancerous fluid in her lungs, a congestive heart condition, irritable bowel syndrome—each sufficient to kill a less vibrant person.

Our conversations in those last years began with her, faint of voice, declaring she would never be well again. As we spoke, her voice would grow stronger, and sometimes she would launch into an arresting and often hilarious narrative, for example about someone who had sent her a six-hundred-page manuscript and then called, screaming with outrage, because Sarton had not yet reported on it. All this time she had the most devoted care from friends around her who responded to her needs with astonishing patience and promptness. Chief among these was Susan Sherman, who for some years literally gave up most of her own life to care for Sarton. I am not sure that Sarton always treated her well, but Sherman's devotion was absolute. She reminded me, as I suspect she reminded Sarton, of "L. M." (Ida Baker), devoted and often scorned "wife" to Katherine Mansfield, although Sarton had no husband to take credit for care he did not provide, and Sherman's attentions were acknowledged by many. I have long been intrigued by the seemingly inevitable arrival, in the lives of single artists, of a much younger acolyte who offers devoted care to the end: one thinks of the companions of Georgia O'Keeffe, Martha Graham, Bertrand Russell. Yet these three acolytes took over the lives of their "masters" even after death, as Sherman did not, except that, as the editor of Sarton's collected letters, she knows more about Sarton's life than anyone, certainly including Sarton.

I offered no such devotion. I offered little, indeed, except what I think May Sarton would have recognized as disinterested (to use that sadly disappearing word, which means, of course, having no personal stake in, which does *not* mean without interest) counsel. My infatuation with her solitude had long since vanished. I early realized that, as a mother and professional worker, I was not alone in envying her her reclusive life, and that, furthermore, she idealized families inordinately. She wrote in *Journal of a Solitude* that "there is something wrong when solitude such as mine can be 'envied' by a happily married woman with children." Her mistake, here, was not in perceiving that anything is "wrong," but in failing to perceive that whether one chooses family or solitude, the price, as I said to her once, is everything. Sarton, for example, did not enjoy watching movies alone on her VCR, whereas a small poll of my own suggests that most married women prefer to watch movies alone, though they scarcely like to say so. As she came slowly to realize, her life as she had evoked it in her books appeared ideal to others, and they sought to imitate her and, if they could not become part of her life, to become her.

I came to understand, further, that her solitude was in fact more invaded than not. People were always coming and going; she was forever cooking for them—she was an excellent cook—and having to put up people she had impulsively invited, or whom she could not turn away. My life, as it turned out, was magnificently solitary compared to hers. I might have children and husband and parents and work, but beyond those boundries there was solitude; if I could find it, I could be assured of my ability to bask in it.

From the time I met her until her death in 1995, she remained a constant thread through my life, an individual unlike any other I knew, cranky, kind, endlessly complaining, meticulously observant. I believe that if Sarton had not been so ill in her last years—"I may die within the next few days or hours," she wrote in *Encore: A Journal of the Eightieth Year*—if life had not seemed so hopeless, she would have achieved a kind of beauty in old age that was, given her illnesses, denied her. Although never conventionally beautiful, she was attractive in a European way, that is, individually striking and in no way resembling a movie actress or model. She never failed to be, for me, as she was for her many readers, an invaluable gift, that rare being: a unique person. She lived a life that, from her first steps into adulthood, veered sharply from mine, granting her experiences I could never have imagined, let alone undertaken. She made outrageous demands on life which life, though it withheld the cheaper sort of fame, allowed her.

Much about Sarton was selfish and even at times pitiless. She fell in love too often and not wisely, and did not always treat those who loved her, or who were devoted to her, with even moderate consideration. Her rages and her infidelities could be injurious. Yet in thinking over her life, I am aware that her transgressions are far easier to narrate, to remember, and to regret than whatever it was that made her uniquely valuable. She was able to arouse affection so often, so deeply, and so widely because she offered affection with so lavish a hand, and with so much humor and attention and excitement. She needed people, and was able to make that need evident; in fulfilling it, therefore, individuals, even if raged at, understood that they had served her in a meaningful way. Her "solitary" life, that is, her life without children or constant companion, was made far from isolated by the great number of people she attracted to her. That attraction, I think, was made up not only of the life and personality she attributed to herself in her writings—more generous and amiable than her true self—but to a kind of gaiety, an ability intensely to experience every moment and to convey that intensity in such a way as to enrich the lives of more sober folk.

Sarton is gone, and yet she seems to be with me as well as lost: I can still hear her voice on the telephone, the way she said "Carol," with a European lilt, rolling the *r*, and with emphasis sharply on the first syllable. Although she knew that I hardly shared her passion for flowers, and had never planted a garden, she sent me two dozen roses each year on my birthday. Even I, who sometimes felt, unfairly and impatiently, that flowers featured perhaps too frequently in her journals, recognized the unusual beauty and endurance of those roses and delighted in them. They flourished, those roses; they had a delicate, delicious scent; they did not, like most cut flowers, seem intent on dying soon after arrival. And their memory, like that of Sarton herself, endures. I still hear her laughter, and tales of woe about her house, which seemed, as houses will, to have determined to enrage her. She returns to me, as I glance through her journals and poetry, whole, aquiver with complaints and courage, vital as she was before her body defeated her.

ENGLAND

with its baby rivers and little towns, each with its
    abbey or its cathedral
with voices—one voice perhaps, echoing through the
    transept.

—MARIANNE MOORE, *"England"*

ENGLAND FOR ME is a country of dreams, long established in my mind and heart, yet always changing. My
mother was reading *To the Lighthouse* shortly after I
was born; she herself visited England when I was very
young and told me of it in different stories, offered at
different times about different places. She and I would
have traveled together to England when I was thirteen,
but Hitler decided otherwise. The English novelists
were her standby, a constant in a life of passionate,
exploratory reading. When she died, I inherited a set
not only of the novels of Thomas Hardy, her favorite
of them all, but also of the writings of George Moore,
an eccentric taste. This set sits in our hall bookcase,
handsome in three-cornered Levant, unread, outdated,
I think, even to her, yet chief among my lares and
penates.

My first trip to England was in 1950; it was as

though I had come home. To visit Bath, where I had lived with Jane Austen, was more return than revelation. London had not yet recovered from the bombings; food was still rationed, or at any rate scarce, and all was shabby. I wanted to stay in England, to live there, but my husband was unalterably American, and he was right. For him, America was the country for us to live in, a country we both knew as home; my England was a fantasy, composed from all the books I read, and the poetry, and the biographies (none of them until recently quite honest, unless you knew how to read between the lines, which I certainly did not). I cannot, even now, imagine what possible life I might have made for myself there, a stranger, after all, with no acquaintances of flesh and blood.

I was to visit England, lovely visits both times, to stay with my then publisher, Livia Gollancz, first in Ladbroke Grove and then in Hampstead. The tall, narrow house in Ladbroke Grove (rather like Lytton Strachey's Lancaster Gate in miniature) had only one WC, in the basement; the guest room was on the top floor. The Hampstead house was quite different, larger, more comfortable, with facilities more wisely placed. (I used it as a setting in one of my detective novels). Livia Gollancz, a wonderful character who used also to visit us in New York, bicycled, when at home, to her allotment where she grew the vegetables on which she largely lived. The allotments were for people in council houses, but could be claimed by outsiders if renounced by the houses' occupants.

As it turned out, however, I was not until my sixties to meet the "real" England, that is, a group of English people who totally conformed to my English fantasies and regaled me with English family life and mild English madness. I encountered them with an English friend, now living in America, whom I had met in my late fifties. She is someone whose delectable English manners and stories happily foreshadowed the family from which she had derived, although she herself is sanity personified. (Patricia Moyes portrayed a mad English family in one of her elegant detective novels; this family, based in some ways on her own, had, she once reported to me, to be moderated in the interests of believability.) My "real" English family is, by happy chance for someone as submerged in English literature as I, descended from a remarkably famous English preacher and author whose portrait, in the National Portrait Gallery, shows him to have passed on to his descendants, if not his religious beliefs or his literary genius, his nose; he has also bequeathed them—as I, who came to know them more than three hundred years after his death, can testify—a countenance reflecting seemly, if raucous, enjoyment. They could not have been nicer or more welcoming to me, and for the first time I experienced with what skill the English, when so inclined, proffer hospitality. I had learned of this particular English talent from reading the letters of Virginia Woolf, her sister Vanessa Bell, and their circle: people endlessly visited, stayed, talked, ate, their presence embraced with great constancy and few complaints.

By the time of my sixties, all my illusions about England had been defeated almost to the point of extinction. The harsh facts of English imperialism, colonialism, racism, sexism, anti-Semitism, classism, homophobia, and xenophobia had been revealed to me. This, I suspect, was inevitable after World War II, but certainly definitive by the 1980s; my by then much more diverse-in-origin graduate students had elaborately delineated for me all these failings of the British Empire. I had also been instructed by the novels of contemporary English authors, and by anecdotes illustrating how ignorant many of the English were of their own literature. A friend reported that an older family member, a "ruler" of Burma before World War II, on being asked if he had met Eric Blair (George Orwell), responded, "Oh, yes, odd fellow; wrote, didn't he?" And Hermione Lee, researching her biography of Virginia Woolf, reported going to view Talland House in Cornwall where Virginia Woolf had spent her happiest childhood days. The present owners of Talland House had, when they bought it, "never heard of the bloody woman," but soon found themselves with "Americans in the living room! Australians in the bathroom!" And yet, and yet, something of that first fascination with writings by the English remained, like the aroma of a lost love, pure, fabricated, and enchanting.

What I loved about England apart from its literature—although that is not unlike saying what one admired about Mozart apart from his music—was its countryside, its neatness, everything described by its poets, from Gray's "Now fades the glimmering landscape on the sight / And all the air a solemn stillness holds" to Hopkins's "Landscape plotted and pieced— fold, fallow, and plough" to Wordsworth's "Hedgerows, hardly hedgerows, little lines of sportive wood run wild."

The English affection for double negatives, exemplified above in the phrase about Mozart, has never left me. Litotes is not the same as bald statement. Even Chaucer and Shakespeare, it is true, used double negatives incorrectly hoping to produce a positive, as when Shakespeare's Claudius says of Hamlet: "Nor what he spoke, though it lacked form a little / Was not like madness." Both Fowler and Sir Ernest Gowers—England's established grammarians—warn firmly against the double negative. As Gowers puts it: "Always avoid multiple negatives when you can. Even if you dodge the traps they set and succeed in saying what you mean, you give your reader a puzzle to solve in sorting the negatives out." (Advice applicable only to those who have not brooded upon English writings, replete with double negatives, all their lives.)

Unless while standing and looking across an English valley you respond as wine connoisseurs are said to do to a rare vintage, you cannot understand what England does, and did, to me. There is, in addition, the fact that everything grows there, that their climate is often misty, rainy, and chilly (weather dear to my heart), and that they write better and perform better upon the stage and in films than any other peoples. I do not dismiss the glories of France, Italy, and the rest of the world; they simply do not speak to me and my passions in the same way. (It is, of course, always possible that since I have no talent whatever for languages, I sensibly decided early to fall in love with a country whose language I had spoken from birth.)

I had had, with my husband, one other memorable visit to England long ago, before Bloomsbury became so prominent. It was some years after I had published a biography of the English Garnett family: Richard, who ran the reading room in the British Museum; Edward, the editor of Conrad, Lawrence, and many others; Constance, who translated Russian novels into English with immense effect; and Edward and Constance's son, David, whom we now visited when he was living in a houseboat on the Thames.

David Garnett, upon being asked about the well-being of Duncan Grant, the painter with and lover of Vanessa Bell, told us that "poor" Duncan Grant didn't sell a picture, and would not we go down to Charleston where he was living and buy one. We went, were asked to tea by Quentin and Olivier Bell who were staying there at the time (this was before they had had more than enough of visiting American scholars) and bought our self-portrait of Duncan Grant. This visit was gratifying, and not alone because we paid far less for a Duncan Grant than one would pay now; the price, even then, though low, was beyond us, if not absolutely beyond us. The gratification lay in our having tea with an English family in a house, Charleston, full of decorations by Vanessa Bell and Duncan Grant, alive with their art and memories of all their talented visitors. Yet there was a formality throughout, as there had always been between me and the English, and though the kindness shown us was great, I could never have the illusion of, in any sense, being part of the Charleston ambience; I was a foreigner.

The family who welcomed me so gloriously in my sixties were still (in my no doubt juvenile and unrealistic view) absolutely English. They ate spotted dick for dessert, they provided English breakfasts—bacon, sausage, eggs, grilled tomato, toast, butter, marmalade—the absolutely best meal, in my opinion, served anywhere at any time. (Agatha Christie's biographer Gillian Gill has noted that Christie survived healthily to eighty-five on a high-cholesterol diet.) But these were only the superficial things. My newly discovered family lived near Regent's Park in a part of London full of history; the lovely houses had mostly been converted to offices, but their exteriors remained the same. We walked in Regent's Park, dazzled by a garden of roses named for Queen Mary blooming with extravagant redolence, and in the Regent's Park Zoo we watched as the elephants bathed on schedule, caressing each other, splashing like children, and, like well-brought-up English children, leaving the pool on command

and carrying their pails in their trunks back to their house.

The "we" who watched the elephants bathe were my English friend and I; she was the source of this late, effervescent experience. This time I had come to England not alone but accompanied by my English friend who returned to visit her original, English family frequently and happily. She took me with her to see and hear for myself these English "characters" she had so often described. It helped, no doubt, that from the beginning I saw them through her eyes, with love. Her family welcomed me and talked with me for hours, sitting around the table, encouraging me to relish—it was June—English tomatoes and English strawberries. With this friend I lunched in pubs on steak and kidney pie or plowman's platter—cheese, bread, pickles—and a glass of English bitter.

My friend's family had not only a large London house on an elegant street but also a summer "cottage" about an hour away. The two of us traveled one weekend on the train to the station nearest to the cottage, and were met by her brother in a car exactly my age. Reconditioning old cars is a family avocation—*hobby* hardly expresses their passion—and this particular open chariot in which we raced home, me holding on to my hat and my seat for dear life, allowed me to feel exactly like a character in a Scott Fitzgerald novel. Considering that I was well past sixty, of generous proportions, with gray hair and spectacles, this was no mean accomplishment on the part of this particular vehicle and its driver. Various other members of the family fixed ancient clocks, collected old china, and tended to have innumerable lamps and other such objects, picked up at antique markets on the off chance that someone in the family might one day need just such an item. They were singular, and warm, and full of laughter; even the grandchildren, with their lilting English voices, seemed figures in a magic garden rather than tiresome brats. I can still hear a small girl's voice, echoing in the garden, calling out to offer us "tea" in tiny china cups.

As Virginia Woolf wrote to Vita Sackville-West, "You always run up against poetry in England." Woolf was being playful, countering Sackville-West's exultant description of Persia, but she was right all the same. Every place sprang up before my eyes as described in some poem or novel or play. Once at Stonehenge—which, I hear, they no longer let you approach—I saw Hardy's Tess, lying there asleep on the sacrificial stone. Later, there were the daffodils in March in Cornwall. We have all seen daffodils "fluttering and dancing in the breeze," but Wordworth's lines (or, perhaps more properly, his sister Dorothy's perceptions transformed by him into a poem), acquire a whole new reality if recalled while one actually watches English daffodils wildly dance. And are there nightingales anywhere but England (though I have not heard one sing in Berkeley Square, never having been with someone I loved in that square in the right season)?

Since I am, obviously, so besotted an Anglophile,

since I have loved England since childhood, and read my own children primarily English books, Beatrix Potter and Alice and Pooh and Mary Poppins, why did I not feel altogether at home in England before that visit in my sixties? Because, of course, reality intruded, and because there was no one to welcome me into an English family, one in which, coming as I did, an attachment of a family member, I was simply included and, apart from their indulgence of my dietary passions, taken altogether for granted. We did not discuss politics, or feminism, or race, or class. If we had, I should no doubt have returned to my earlier suspicions of English life, had English prejudice been recalled to me in a way I could no longer ignore. What did we talk of? I can hardly remember; only the laughter, the generosity, the *Englishness* remains with me. It was as though a lover, who had turned into a Republican, eager to beat down the poor, business-driven, sexist, had reappeared and we had somehow been able to capture all the passion, knowing we would not have time enough for philosophy too.

Not only children's books had kept England in my mind's eye but also detectives who haunted their accustomed environs, from Baker Street where Sherlock Holmes had rooms, to Piccadilly where Dorothy Sayers's Peter Wimsey lived, to Mecklenberg Square where Sayers's Harriet Vane moved after she was acquitted of murdering her lover, to the old Scotland Yard where Josephine Tey's Inspector Alan Grant and Ngaio Marsh's Inspector/Superintendent Roderick Alleyn hung out, to New Scotland Yard, headquarters for P. D. James's Commander Adam Dalgliesh. All of these detectives (except, of course, Harriet Vane) belonged to gentlemen's clubs.

For years I had read of those English clubs, male fortresses, more resistant even than the House of Lords to the infiltration of females. One of the women detective story writers I had met (but only in New York, for drinks in the Algonquin Hotel lobby) was one of the females that the Reform Club, true to its name and its tradition, had lately allowed to become members. My friend and I tiptoed in, peeking even into the reading room where irritable-looking men in huge leather chairs, exactly as they had always been pictured, rattled newspapers over which they glared at us, we thought unhappily. Undaunted, we took seats on a leather couch and ourselves consulted newspapers. A blissful moment. Then, out of that intimidating room to the large entrance hall where drinks were being served, and our detective writer friend introduced us to a man who gallantly bought all three of us "ladies'" drinks. He turned out to be quite a conservative fellow, but we debated him only in the mildest of ways as we consumed the single malt scotch he had bestowed upon us.

Our detective-writing woman should be identified. Her name is Sarah Caudwell, and she has written three (alas only three so far) of the most dazzling English detective novels extant. You can almost hear her very English voice, and indeed she bears a remarkable resemblance to one of her characters, though not her detective, a brilliant, rather mercurial woman with a taste for handsome men on the right side of forty. Sarah herself speaks the purest upper-class English, which is to say that it is not always absolutely decipherable, and is made even more elusive by her constant smoking of a pipe. Her beautiful hands are often tarnished with nicotine or smudges from the spent wooden matches with which she has lit her steadily expiring pipe. For me, who once wrote on Christopher Isherwood, she is especially notable for being the daughter of "Sally Bowles," a character made famous in Isherwood's *Berlin Stories,* and most readily recognized as the protagonist of *Cabaret.* Sarah feels that her mother was traduced by Isherwood, and I am inclined to agree, except that he rendered Sally Bowles as amusing and intelligent, like Sarah.

On this visit, in my sixties, I, so to speak, truly came home. I visited the House of Lords, the guest of P. D. James, and the Reform Club, the guest of Sarah Caudwell. Virago, my English publisher, had brought me over for a bit of promotion—the English are mild in their promotional demands; in addition, I attended a detective writers' conference in Nottingham, replete with Robin Hood.

But it was my friend who made the journey memorable, whose family evoked an Englishness that would hardly endure for long. Friendship was the key and the great gift of my sixties. I was, in fact, fifty-

seven when I met this friend, and have rejoiced to find
that blessing properly articulated by W. H. Auden:

At twenty we find our friends for ourselves, but it
   takes Heaven
To find us one when we are fifty-seven.

SEX AND ROMANCE

[There is] a narrative difficulty which will always be acute: how to attach a heterosexual emotional life to a character whose strength comes from her transcendence of usual sexual roles?

—HERMIONE LEE, *Willa Cather: Double Lives*

I CANNOT QUITE cure myself of the conviction that if we could discover a word that meant "adventure" and did not mean "romance," we in our late decades would be able to free ourselves from the compulsion always to connect yearning and sex. If an ancient (by American standards) woman finds herself longing for something new, something as yet not found, must that something always be sex or till-death-do-us-part romance? The reason for the predominence of sexual aspiration, I have decided, is that no other adventure has quite the symbolic force, not to mention the force of the entire culture, behind it. Elder hostels at colleges and overplanned excursions to foreign parts hardly suggest the éclat of a new experience, and our society offers us who are old nothing but the same promises it holds out, with only slightly more sanity, to the young.

An example leapt out at me from a recent issue of *The New York Times Book Review*. Kate Muir, described as the Paris features writer of *The Times* of London, had been allowed an entire page to write about *Desert Queen*, Janet Wallach's biography of Gertrude Bell. Bell was an intrepid traveler and diplomat of the early twentieth century whose influence on Middle Eastern affairs was profound. She had courage, energy, and intelligence, and lived an extraordinary life for her time, perhaps even for ours. But the reviewer ends on a pitying note:

The only man who proposed to her was vetoed by her parents as too poor and unsuitable. She had a romance with a married man, largely conducted by letter, that was never consummated. Another relationship during her 50's dwindled away into friendship.

As Ms. Muir bemoans Bell's "lack of success as a woman in personal relationships," she could not be more offtrack if she had worked on it with both hands for a fortnight. There is not a single implication in this judgment of Gertrude Bell or of any woman with which I agree. A romance with a married man, accomplished in letters and "unconsummated," is accounted as sad, but not half so sad as a relationship with a man that is allowed to *"dwindle away* into friendship." This is a particularly silly statement and poor advice to those of us advancing in years. Nearer the truth is the fact that if an older woman's relationship to a man has not dwindled (I would say developed) into friendship, it has either continued as a weekly sexual rite (possible, if improbable) or (more likely) been dissipated altogether.

It certainly seems true that Gertrude Bell suffered a "broken heart" when young because her father would not let her marry her young man; Muir goes on to suggest that Bell might have had a fuller life if her parents had not interfered and she had married "the poor, unsuitable chap." What the definition of a "fuller life" might, in the case of Gertrude Bell, possibly have been eludes me; no doubt it would have been nicer if she could have enjoyed both sex and the Middle East, but Muir's implication is clearly that the former would have been the wiser choice. I am reminded how for many years we have heard how Clara Wieck's wicked father actually tried to stop her from marrying Robert Schumann, fearing it would be the end of her career as a highly regarded pianist and composer. Foolish, antiromantic Papa, standing in the way of true love. So Clara married Robert, bore eight children, nursed Robert through his breakdowns, and spent the years after he was institutionalized playing his music (some of which she may have written) all over Europe to keep his name before the public. She had no time for her own musical ambitions, but a woman's professional life is always considered well lost for love. But need we always mourn the lack of enduring love when, in hindsight, we consider the life of an accomplished woman?

This is not to deny that Gertrude Bell might have agreed with Ms. Muir; when the regime she had worked to establish in Iraq was in place, she found herself without a political role and no longer a person of importance in the realm where she had so long influenced events. Purposeless, and alone, she died at almost fifty-eight, having taken rather too many sleeping pills before retiring (without, however, having indicated any intention of suicide to her friends). The man she wanted to marry did not want to marry her; it happens. But was her sadness due only to her failure in love, or also, perhaps mainly, to her loss of position and influence? Bell's mind, as with the minds of many of us, may indeed have latched on to the conjugally disinclined man as the cause of misery; it was the symbol of the failure of aging that society offered her, as it offers all of us, neatly packaged and ready for easy consumption.

Bell's recent biography, far from escaping this pitfall, dotes upon it. Selina Hastings, writing in *The New Yorker,* suggests (unlike Ms. Muir) that perusing *Desert Queen* is like "reading two books simultaneously; one a highly intelligent history of the Middle East, the other a Harlequin romance." She might have added that almost every aging unmarried woman's life is inevitably viewed in the light of this dichotomy.

I have said that all of us who are aging, and particularly us aging women, will do well to listen to the young often and earnestly. But we must never, never listen to them on the subject of sex. They are useful on this subject only to one eager to gather information on esoteric techniques and not-altogether-usual practices. The young are inclined to think, at least if they are heterosexual, that any woman who doesn't end up with a man in a long, clearly "consummated," relationship is a failure, even if, like Gertrude Bell, she is responsible for most of today's conditions in the Middle East.

We often hear that the old are absorbed, indeed compelled, by their interest in sex, and that it is cruel to deprive them of this compulsion, or to mock it. I'm told by a friend who garnered the fact in the print media—he can't quite remember where—that the largest-selling large-print book was *Sex After Sixty*. (Which reminds me of a Gloria Steinem remark, made as she put on her reading glasses to present a paper to an enormous gathering: "You know you're getting on when you have to put on reading glasses to make love.") I'm not saying that the old may not be, or should not be, as active sexually as fate and inclination allow. But I am going out on a limb here to declare that it is likely that aging women who have had a career of adventure and accomplishment, even acclaimed writers who are aging, still find themselves at as great a loss to come up with a late adventure that is not romance.

Two famous women novelists of today emphatically disagree with me when it comes to dreams of romantic sex in the later years; they have both written novels to assure us that professionally successful women in their late fifties or sixties may fall into desperate desire for a man and for sexual passion. In my view, these novelists have internalized, or failed to expunge, youthful society's unchanging homage to romance. They might well answer, in their turn, that resistance to romance at any age is not humanly possible. Marilyn French's *My Summer with George* and Doris Lessing's *Love, Again* each has this theme at its center. Here is Lessing:

I'm sick, she said to herself. "You're sick." I'm sick with love, and that is all there is to it. How could such a thing have happened? What does Nature think it is up to? (Eyeball to eyeball with Nature, elderly people often accuse it—her?—of ineptitude, of sheer incompetence.) I simply can't wait to get back to my cool, elderly self, all passion spent.

And here is French (her heroine is talking to women friends):

"I thought I had had a happy life until I met him. I thought I had a great life, the life I'd always wanted. It's just that meeting him triggered something. You know— the happily-ever-after button? And what is so upsetting is discovering how powerful it is. After all these years. After all those husbands and even more lovers . . . I never had this fantasy before [ellipses French's]."

Both protagonists of these novels have had husbands, lovers, children. Lessing's heroine is besieged by sexual passion for first one, then another man. French's protagonist desires a man she has met, hoping for lasting relationship; as she observes, "till death do you part" isn't so long when you're in your sixties. Both authors are highly skilled writers, intelligent women, and both have been known as feminists, though Lessing appears to no longer welcome that designation. Why are they promoting romance in their leading ladies' later years? (French herself is in her sixties, Lessing in her seventies.)

Why indeed? There are three possible explanations. One: These authors are simply accurate in their assumptions, so why shouldn't they write about them? Two: They may be on drugs—that is, hormones. Three: Successful as they are, they have been caught up in the romantic story with which all of us are pummeled, day and night, everywhere we go, whatever we do. Romance, at any age, is ubiquitously boosted as the best game in town.

I suspect that number three is the answer. But why should Lessing and French, or their protagonists, all highly successful women, fall victim to the current, invasive environment of romance? My guess is that women whose lives are professionally successful, and who have all they want of life's material blessings and furnishings, often find themselves overcome by a desire for something—risk, adventure, a new challenge—they know not exactly what. And today's proliferation of the romantic story stands ready to answer that craving or need. But how can a fiction writer name another resolution, when our culture offers none? Nor can I, in exactly this situation, even after much cogitation, suggest a satisfactory resolution to this powerful dilemma.

Perhaps another reason is that among those whom Lessing's heroine, with more accuracy than tact, calls "the elderly," those who have found that sex has lost its habit of robust and constant insistence rarely have the fortitude to admit it. Few publicly claim relief in their later years, as did Sophocles, from enslavement to sex, that demanding master. Marilyn French offers what may indeed be the best explanation we can come up with at this moment for the phenomenon of women's late desires. The mated, she suggests, often wish intensely for unfettered liberty, while the un-mated long for the joys, real or imagined, of extended intimacy. Hers is a marvelously cogent clarification of this continuing dilemma, and suggests that what we have here is a basic condition of being human—that is, to want with fervency the exact opposite of what one has. My only response would be to hope that companionship might be both desired and gained apart from fantasies of either sex or romance.

Only a few novelists, past and present, have cele-brated what Ms. Muir bemoans: a relationship with a man that "dwindles" into friendship. Writers as di-verse as Sand, Anne Brontë, Hardy, Cather, have marked a woman's reaching maturity with her realiza-tion that to love your male friend is the rarest and most satisfying of blessings. Even some current novelists have caught on to this. Susan Isaacs in her recent *Lily White* affirms the advantage of friendship over passion, even though she has hitherto authored novels unalterably romantic, however intelligent. Similarly, P. D. James, in *Original Sin,* offers this paragraph about a man a woman will, at the end of the novel, learn to cherish:

She could marry James de Witt and move into his charming house in Hillgate Village and have his children, the children she, too, wanted. She could rely on his love, be certain of his kindness, know that, whatever problems their marriage might bring, there would be no cruelty and no rejection. She might have taught herself, not to desire him, since that was not susceptible to the will, but to find in kindness and gentleness a substitute for desire, so that in time sex with him would become possible, even agreeable, at its lowest a belief that love could in time beget love.

The problem James's character is facing here is that she has for three months been the lover of a wholly selfish man who has rejected her, leaving her with the knowledge of how exciting sex with a skillful, unfettered man can be. This troubles her for most of the book, but in the end she happily claims James de Witt.

I have heard women mention their sorrow at having married men they did not love. But in almost every case, it turns out that what is lacking is not only palpitating desire for the husband but also any sense of him as a friend, as someone who can be conversed with readily and often. In *Writing a Woman's Life* I divided men, rather too taxonomically, into lovers and husbands, and I've taken a lot of flak for it. What I neglected to mention is that one may feel overwhelming desire for a man with whom the relationship can "dwindle" (that is, develop) into friendship. It sometimes happens: people do win the lottery. But if obsessive desire and skillful technique are the only basis for the woman's devotion, even that, should she and the man marry, will inevitably become less compelling once it is given full range in the marriage bed. The craving for the sexually skillful lover is almost always abetted by the infrequency of meetings with him. In short, I suggest that the "elderly" leave romance to the young, and welcome friendship. In all the novels I have mentioned—by Cather, Hardy, et al.—which end in the powerful friendship between a man and a woman, the woman has first thrown her hat over the mill at a "romantic" man. This, of course, is an adventure suitable only to the young, or to the aged who wish to suffer forever the plight of unsatisfied sexual passion. Both French's and Lessing's protagonists end up alone, their sane, sensible, intelligent selves, harried but not lost.

Life, even long ago, has occasionally celebrated the elegance of a passion that becomes friendship. My daughter Margaret, who has a deep admiration for Diderot and who likes, in her words, to "pepper you with Diderot now and then," tells me (via e-mail) that he "had a passionate—intellectually passionate—relationship with Sophie Volland, from when he was forty-five and she was forty-three until her death four months before his own. He wrote her many fascinating letters, clearly treating her as his intellectual equal, and remaining interested in her thoughts. No one has ever been certain if they slept together." I suspect that Diderot and Volland saw no reason to discuss in their letters whether or not they slept together or for how long, or to reveal it to others; the evidence of their friendship has endured, however, because (I assume) they recognized that there was nothing shameful about it, nor that it was less than it might have been.

Am I able to suggest a substitute, unromantic adventure for women's later life? No, alas, I am not, although I have considered the matter long and hard. I do believe, however, that as we women reach our later years, sex, if it is part of our lives, is a by-product, not the dominant element. Like happiness, or beauty in a work of art, sex after sixty cannot be the object of any undertaking, though it may sometimes be a wonderful and unsought-for result. Whatever the satisfying and as yet culturally endorsed adventure after sixty may be, its necessary element is the sense of something essential and vital having been achieved or discovered or learned. (I *do* wish I could say this in a sexier way.)

MEMORY

Would but some wingéd Angel ere too late
Arrest the yet unfolded Roll of Fate,
    And make the stern Recorder otherwise
Enregister, or quite obliterate!

—EDWARD FITZGERALD, *The Rubáiyát of Omar Khayyám*

HAD I BEEN GRANTED one wish for my later years, it would have been for the obliteration of the instant, contiguous memory. No one would choose to lose the valuable fruits of her long experience, but this, in fact, is more a matter of history than of memory; to put it another way, experience, once we have processed it, becomes a part of our present consciousness and can no longer properly be called memory at all. Nor, perhaps, would we wish to lose remembrance of happy or funny occasions from our past. Yet, often, such pleasant reminiscences have formed themselves into a frozen anecdote, no longer vital and, because forever encased in the amber of repetition, unable to offer to us as we recall or recount it any new rewards. I have come to believe that the cost of memory in later life is high, perhaps prohibitively so. Has anyone tried to determine the cause, at sixty or even earlier, of the involuntary return of usually inconsequential memories?

Here is an example: I am walking, sometime in my sixties, and talking with a friend when, glancing at the sidewalk, I see a coin. I stoop to pick it up, and am flooded with a memory. I am three years old, walking behind my parents along a pleasant street. I spy a dime on the sidewalk and stopping, attempt to grasp it. But I am wearing angora mittens, and cannot capture the dime. At the age of three, I do not know what the coin is worth, but I know it is money. My parents, looking back, return to where I am and retrieve the dime for me. I am told that I can buy what I like with it— dimes bought a great deal more in those days—and I know exactly what I want. I had seen a cat balloon in a newspaper store on the corner of our street; after the balloon was blown up, the mouth was knotted and inserted into cardboard feet so that the cat stood. This wholly happy memory has, of course, taken me far longer to describe than it took for it to assert itself, entire, into my consciousness. I suspect that dreams we remember on waking, dreams that seemed to have absorbed us all night, are really the stuff of mere seconds before we awaken.

I did not invite that memory, but it was a harbinger of others to follow. None of mine were significant of anything; they had simply been called forth by some process of association which I have come to believe is activated only in our later years, and which, if not carefully monitored, can evolve into the ultimate temptation of one's last decades. That temptation is to recall grudges, to dwell on ancient wrongs and miseries and betrayals, to allow these memories, if they are not properly controlled, to dominate thought and therefore life. A friend, not herself a mother, hoisting a chubby six-month-old baby, recalls her younger sister, how "gushy" (her word) the sister felt to her when touched on the belly, and how bitterly she resented this intruder. The pain of that resentment is as strong as ever, and joins other lingering hostilities against her mother. Even if involuntary memories are, like mine, benign, they threaten to encourage the reappearance of others, and, worse, to suggest that dwelling upon such memories may be in some way productive. In my view, it rarely is.

May Sarton, in her later years, complained bitterly and often that both her biographer and the editor of her letters insistently thrust upon her memories she did not want to face or relive or even recall. It had apparently not occurred to her that people who devote themselves to recounting, in whatever form, the story of your life will remind you of the past—will, if they are biographers, insist upon reminding you.

In my sixties, I found myself similarly asked to recall the past: a professor of English was writing *my* biography, although happily she was willing to confine herself to what she called my intellectual and professional life. This was to be an account of a feminist, older than most, who had therefore had the chance to experience the new women's movement in academia earlier than the majority of women professors. Her motive was to provide one thread in what would inevitably become a much larger tapestry.

I was fortunate in that my biographer evoked only innocuous memories. Indeed, without her I would not have learned that Simone de Beauvoir had visited Wellesley while I was a student there and had apparently decided she had nothing to say to me. At the time I had no idea who she was. *The Second Sex* was published three or four years later in France, and not in the United States until almost ten years after her Wellesley visit. Still, I was glad to discover that I had been within range of her, even if that knowledge provided only a memory missed. (Later, I read in her autobiography of her scorn, during what I assume was the same American visit, of the elaborate dinner parties given by American women. "Why don't they get a drink in a bar and then go to a restaurant?" she intelligently wondered—or words to that effect. She was obviously a woman whom I might have claimed as a model had I known of her earlier.)

Sarton wept over old memories. Gloria Steinem, on the contrary, was not distracted by them, except when actually confronted with Toledo, Ohio, and the scenes of her childhood there; these she found unbearable. The poet Maxine Kumin, full of memories, seems less captured by them than evoking them for the sake of her poetry (a quite different matter), although if a memory offered, she has not always declined to indulge it, as some of her poetry testifies. I, strangely devoid of either memory or desire to change the past—except as with the suicide of a friend, and such events are blessedly rare—have become a victim of the epidemic of memory only in a casual, instantaneous way. Perhaps because of the example of Sarton, and also because of my own mother's torture by recollection, I have been able happily to remain in the present.

Certain memories would rise in my mother's mind in the last twenty or so years of her life—she died when she was seventy-seven—and she would seem to suffer over and over again from the unfairness, the injustice, of what she recalled: how, as a child, she had been left to watch over smaller siblings and cousins; how she had had no one to ask about her math problems in high school; how she had hated leaving her job in a bank to marry. So May Sarton, in the last television interview she gave shortly before her death, reverted to her still fierce outrage at a monstrous review of her collected poems long decades ago. Not even the interviewer, any more than I through the long years, could rescue her from her contemplation of past miseries.

One reason I may have escaped memory's thrall was a revelation of how individual, therefore unreliable, are memories. On one of my husband's and my big anniversaries, our children decided to recall, in the presence of some old friends, events of their childhood. They were all happy events, or ones complimentary to their father and me—we were, after all, the subjects of this celebration—and it was only that night that my husband and I admitted to each other that we could hardly remember any of these vivid recollections. Our children have since discovered that even they, very close to one another in age, do not remember the same things, or not in the same way.

What one remembers is, I think, a clue to what one wants to be. I turned my back on involuntary memories, and refused to give them more than passing attention, because I did not wish to be a rememberer; I cannot see the reason for it. I suspect that I am extreme in this; autobiographical fictions of childhood and backward-reaching memoirs certainly abound, as though the writers were trying not only to turn early memory into art but even to chase it as far back as it would lead. My eccentricity here will be confirmed by the confession that I have no interest in dreams, particularly my own. They always seem to me the detritus of the mind, what could not be satisfactorily processed during the day.

And there is another reason why memory seems to me an untrustworthy ally. The detective stories I write under the name Amanda Cross are often assumed to be autobiographical, to arise from memory and desire, which they do not. When I portrayed some fictional members of the Harvard English department, no one believed they were not portraits of actual Harvard faculty. In fact, as I had plainly stated in a note at the front of the book, I knew no one in that department except one man who had moved there from Columbia, and he was not in my novel. Nonetheless, the conviction that these characters were based on life

persisted. I came to understand this only with the real-
ization, which was some years in coming, that all
pompous, self-satisfied, established male professors
have similar characteristics; if you have described one,
you have described many. No harm came to me from
this particularly misunderstanding, but Sarton long
dwelt on the memory of Harry Levin's conviction that
he was portrayed as the Jewish professor in her novel
Faithful Are the Wounds, set at Harvard, an identifica-
tion she continued to deny. For years she insisted
(without real evidence) that it was he who had prevented her from achieving positions and memberships
that she desired. That memory haunted her, replaying
itself, never responding to analysis, never dismissed.
With age it returned even more frequently, accompanied by ever deeper resentment.

I have by now determined this about recurring
memories: They must either be disregarded or have
their power analyzed away. For me, since memories
seem not to establish powerful holds on my mind,
dismissing them has been the constructive procedure.
This assertion must suggest the need, in my rejection-
of-memory phase, of psychoanalysis or therapy. That I
have never been in therapy seems astonishing to many
people, and may go far to explain my evident peculiar-
ity in abjuring memory in my sixties and beyond. My
avoidance of therapy is, however, a generational one:
in my young adult days, had there been therapists
sympathetic to feminism and with genuine, post-
Freudian understanding of the conflicts in women's

lives, I could certainly have consulted one. There have arisen therapists these days who do not dwell entirely on the client's past but attempt to work on the problems immediately to be faced. Some of these problems will, inevitably, have their roots in early events and conditions, but these are dwelt upon only where the connection is palpable. But the tales of those I knew who were in analysis scared me off (although my first detective novel, *In the Last Analysis,* was highly sympathetic to psychoanalysis, including assent to Freud's abandonment of the seduction theory). After that, I didn't seem to find a need commensurate with the time and money that therapy would have required. My impatience with memory, and my scant portion of nostalgia, may have had something to do with this, as may the fact that my sixties were my happiest time, just as my time of discontent and anxiety was when my children were young, when I felt imprisoned in the domestic life, and when few people, like the male friends with whom I enjoyed discussion, understood or even had patience with a condition like mine.

A young Cambridge undergraduate once praised E. M. Forster, who was then living as an octogenarian in King's College, because, unlike most people of his age, he did not commend the past in comparison to the present, but relished the present and spoke of it in its own terms. The young are bored to tears by accounts of the past; it seems to them always to be recalled as better, or harder, or more honorable than the present. To so discourage the young is foolish; it is wise to make new and younger friends since, as Samuel Johnson understood: "If a man [*sic*] does not make new acquaintances as he advances through life, he will soon find himself left alone." Therefore, not to put off the young, it seems the better part of sense to encourage memories to chase themselves out of consciousness with the same force they have summoned to propel themselves into it.

Ecclesiastes recognized the mark of aging to be when desire fails. Thus Eliot in *The Waste Land* called April the cruelest month, "mixing / Memory and desire," because he knew that desire is most likely to fail when memory and regret combine to defeat it. April, that interstitial month between winter and spring, is the most likely to encourage this dangerous combination.

It was the poet Tennyson, whom Eliot detested, who wrote, "O Death in Life, the days that are no more." As was the wont of Victorians, Tennyson took a little longer achingly to remind us of memories' dangers:

> Tears, idle tears, I know not what they mean,
> Tears from the depth of some divine despair
> Rise in the heart, and gather to the eyes,
> In looking on the happy Autumn-fields,
> And thinking of the days that are no more.

In looking at the happy autumn fields, why turn to thoughts of earlier times and the dirges they inspire? I was told, in my undergraduate days, of a professor of ichthyology who refused to learn the names of his students because every time he learned a student's name he forgot the name of a fish. Similarly, I believe that every time those of us in our last decades allow a memory to occur, we forget to look at what is in front of us, at the new ideas and pleasures we might, if firmly in the present, encounter and enjoy. When a memory assaults me, reminding me of the cat balloon, I forget where I was when I spotted the coin on the sidewalk. Forget, that is, the too readily fleeting present.

ON NOT WEARING
DRESSES

Well-meaning people were affronted by what they considered to be a frightening challenge to the conventions
of the masculine-feminine polarity.

—SUSAN BROWNMILLER, *Femininity*

ONE GLANCE at women's clothing in nineteenth-
century paintings discloses the purposes of these elaborate dresses: to attract attention and hamper movement. From early on, I knew I scorned both
objectives. When, in my young adulthood, newly
awakened Freudians droned on about penis envy, I
recognized that what I envied in men was not their
sexual equipment but their clothes. From comfortable
flat-soled shoes to trousers with deep pockets to cotton
shirts to jackets with many and even inner pockets,
this male attire seemed to be unfairly limited to one
sex. It was clearly, at least in our climate, the most
comfortable outfit possible. It is, therefore, one of the
chief sources in my sixties of sharp, daily joy that I
have the chance at last, without appearing peculiar,
without attracting attention, to wear this oh so satisfying and comfortable clothing formerly forbidden me:

even in the Army and the baseball leagues during World War II, women wore skirts.

I had attained a lifelong ambition. From my adolescence, with garter belts and girdles (I once had to explain to a college class what a girdle was; some of the students recognized my description, having seen their mothers grapple with "one of those"), from stockings to panty hose, from deliberations about the length of dresses and the need of petticoats, I had achieved independence.

I was two years into my sixties when I began to undertake the serious transformation of my wardrobe. I had long been wearing jeans, sweat pants, and other casual attire while working in the confines of my home, but venturing forth, certainly beyond the neighborhood and for any social or professional meeting, I felt impelled to put on proper "womanly" apparel. It had taken the persuasion of my children to allow me to wear trousers at all. Before the days of sweat pants at home, I had hung around the house in my dressing gown; as another working woman friend and I used to joke together, our children taunted us with never going out, since we had on dressing gowns when they left in the morning and had stripped ourselves of panty hose and confining accoutrements and dived back into our comfortable *déshabillé* before the children returned.

In the early days of the feminist movement, when I was invited to deliver a talk I would always dress in a manner designed to assuage any anxiety the audience might have about feminism. I wore what at that time were called Kimberley Knits, quietly elegant, graced with a strand of pearls and delicate earrings; to complete this disguise I of course wore ladylike pumps with midsize heels. It was a mark of the feminist movement's achievements that, by the time I reached the age of sixty, such camouflage was no longer necessary. (We feminists were wont to refer to wearing this camouflage as being "in drag.")

A Smith graduation I attended at age sixty-two marked the last time I wore heels. As they sank into the mud on our way to the academic procession, and my toes could be felt crunching unhappily together, I vowed to wear them no more. I gave away all my shoes with heels and turned to flats. Dresses took a good deal longer to eschew. Although I wore trousers far more often, I would creep unhappily into panty hose and properly feminine garments before giving a speech or attending a required social event.

Since I had also, with maturity, that is, at about fifty-five, given up trying to stay thin, I now needed dresses that would allow for my mid-body expansion without hanging on me like a tent I had mistakenly donned instead of slept in. I turned to catalogs—a lifesaver. But I did not at first realize that the sizes were on a different scale: a 14X bore no relation to the old 14 I had been wearing; thus the first dress I ordered was immense.

"Are you planning to wear it or live in it?" my bewildered husband inquired.

Eventually, I found a dressmaker of modest cost and a blessed willingness to interact with me entirely by mail and phone until the final product was delivered. She made me many highly suitable dresses, as well as pants with tunics to wear above them.

Several years ago, I was staying in a hotel in London. Leaving my room, I would walk to the elevator down a long hall at the end of which was a full-length mirror. Each day, although I had become marvelously talented at not seeing myself in the mirror, even when applying lipstick, I could not help but view my by now quite stately image as it traversed the distance to the elevator. What was soon obvious was that in the dresses I resembled a walking bolster; in my pants and tunic, I was noticeably less bolsterish. At that moment of revelation, I donated my dresses, many quite recently acquired, to a battered women's shelter and determined to wear pants for all occasions. While I could never be called fashionable by anyone in her right mind, at least my clothing was within the confines of the acceptable. I had abjured dresses and, above all, panty hose, discovered catalogs and a dressmaker, and learned to live with the knowledge that whatever I did and wherever I was going, I would be comfortable from my feet up. It was only after this mind-boggling decision that I came across something Susan Brownmiller had written a decade earlier, explaining why she persisted in not wearing skirts or dresses:

Because I don't like this artificial gender distinction. Because I don't wish to start shaving my legs again. Because I don't want to return to the expense and aggravation of nylons. Because I will not reacquaint myself with the discomfort of feminine shoes. Because I'm at peace with the freedom and comfort of trousers. Because it costs a lot less to wear nothing but pants. . . . Because I remember resenting the enormous amount of think time I used to pour into superficial upkeep concerns, and because the nature of feminine dressing is superficial in essence. . . . To care about feminine fashion, and do it well, is to be obsessively involved in inconsequential details on a serious basis. There is no relief. To not be involved is to risk looking eccentric and peculiar, or sloppy and uncared for, or mannish and manhating, or all of the above.

It was only after a time of sartorial bliss that it occurred to me to notice something else about this transformation: I had achieved an androgynous wardrobe. Although my shirts buttoned differently from a man's, and my pants were probably larger in the seat than those worn by most males, my clothes were not, in any absolute sense, "feminine" as opposed to "masculine." They were, at least compared to the highly gendered clothing of my youth and the preceding century, not readily distinguishable from what a man might wear. This, of course, would make a play like *Charley's Aunt* impossible, as it would render cross-dressers more easily detectable. Fortunately for both playwrights and gender-benders, a great many women have remained devoted to short, tight skirts, to high heels, and to peekaboo blouses. One of the ironies of the advent of androgynous dress is that it is far harder now for men to disguise themselves as women than it was formerly. I remember once, years ago, seeing a production of *As You Like It* in modern dress at Stratford in England, and Rosalind wore exactly the same clothes as a woman and as a man. It was a brilliant production.

In 1973, I published a book called *Toward a Recognition of Androgyny*. It is hard now to remember that the word *androgyny* was quite unfamiliar to most people at that time. Androgyny almost immediately became a popular term and a popular idea, but at the time of my book, when not many besides Adrienne Rich had used the word, it was considered shocking. I remember the way my book was damned in the daily *New York Times* by Anatole Broyard, who years later, to my delight, would complain in the same space that androgyny had been insufficiently taken account of by the author of whatever book was under review. Eventually the attention of the media to the term and the concept was so intense (*androgyny* had become a buzzword) that Adrienne Rich, to my sorrow, removed her poem on androgyny from her collected works, published in 1993. We kept hearing about Michael Jackson and Boy George, and certain clever folks even began noticing that the great movie stars from the thirties on were androgynous: Fred Astaire, Greta Garbo, Marlene Dietrich, Cary Grant, Katharine Hepburn.

There were, it also soon turned out, many feminists who didn't much care for the term *androgyny*. Their complaints, apart from its popularization by the media, which is always disturbing to serious people, were, first, that the very word itself underscored that there were two sexes, thus emphasizing the very division that androgyny sought to lessen, and, second, that whenever androgyny had been evoked in the past, from the days of Renaissance paintings to Carl Jung's admonitions to men to encourage their anima, the male was always urged to allow his "female" characteristics to flourish, but females were warned never to permit "male" characteristics to mar their womanliness. These were cogent criticisms.

Oddly, however, in spite of all this, androgyny has endured both as a popular adjective and, more significantly, as a liberating idea. I had suggested, in the face of much of this criticism, that androgyny was most useful as an introductory idea, allowing individuals, particularly individuals struggling for a sense of identity, to contemplate themselves outside of conventional and stereotypical gender expectations. Once a person had ceased to be ashamed of tendencies toward behavior relegated by convention only to the opposite sex, once these tendencies had been recognized as allowable, then he or she—but more often she because the strictures restricting female dress and behavior were more stringent—could begin to conceive of life in a new way. Studies, by Sandra Bem and others, indicated that the less androgynous the person, the likelier he or she was to be incapable of action if the appropriate action was not clearly delineated. (Bem's work on androgyny resulted in the Bem Sex Role Inventory, a widely used instrument in social psychology today.) How many women there were, I used to think, before this women's movement, who tore themselves or their families apart because they could not allow themselves any action or occupation that could appear manly, and might make their husbands appear less so.

With my new liberating clothing, I began to measure my own androgyny, which had been present from earliest childhood, though I had denied it, if decreasingly, until my sixties. I liked male clothing; I liked the freedom of male movement and the right to be an athlete, which girls were not really permitted to be in my youth. (We played basketball on a divided court, limited to three dribbles.) Also, I wanted to have a profession, not just to marry and have children. All that made me androgynous, and I came in my sixties to understand that, oddly enough, clothes had been the last "appropriate" restraint in my life to give way. Oh, the triumph of saying in one's sixties that one will never wear panty hose again.

I do not wish to exaggerate here, nor to suggest that women who enjoy "feminine" clothing are somehow retrograde. That would be simple reversal, and would defeat the whole point of androgyny, and for that matter, of feminism; in both, the whole point is choice. Furthermore, were I in a profession that demanded "feminine" dress I would adopt it as a necessary uniform. Fortunately, most professions now allow for a far wider choice in dress, though I understand there are many situations in which a "power suit" is the only acceptable dress for women.

Happily, I have been able, in my sixties and, I trust, beyond, to gratify my androgynous self. I was, however, surprised recently to be told by a young lesbian friend, with whom Bianca and I were walking, that everyone could tell she was a lesbian by the way she dressed. This stopped me and therefore Bianca in our tracks. "But," I said, "you're not dressed differently from me." We looked each other over. She is slim, and wore a sweater over a shirt, while I was wearing a raincoat over my sweater. We both wore pants and running shoes. She had pierced ears with little gold rings in them; I was earringless (on social occasions, I wear earrings with clips). Her hair was elegantly shaped, mine was pulled back into a bun. I accused her of being stereotypical, but she was certain of the impression she made. "You wear lipstick," she finally announced in triumph. That was true, but I have noticed that most women of my generation, if they wear any makeup at all, wear lipstick. We finally shrugged and continued on our way. Naturally, I began to wonder if androgynous dress is disturbing to the conventional because it may denote homosexuality. I recalled that in the sixties (*the* sixties, not my sixties) some people found it profoundly disturbing not to be able to tell at a glance the sex of young people passing by. If our clothes have been allowed to become more androgynous, perhaps our attitudes toward homosexuality have not been sufficiently reformed. And yet, pondering upon my acquaintances, I was certain, as I told my young friend, that no one could tell the sexual preference of any of them by their clothes. She answered that I just didn't know how to recognize the signs. We left it at that, but I still think I was right. Androgyny defeats semiotics, that is, the signs that give us immediate signals of significance.

Bisexuality is a new term that has recently spread in popular usage. In my sixty-ninth year, I was partly annoyed and partly amused to find that Marjorie Garber, publishing *Vice Versa: Bisexuality and the Eroticism of Everyday Life,* took the occasion to hammer away at me and the idea of androgyny for many pages. My thought at first was that it was quite unfair to berate a living author for a book she wrote twenty-five years ago without asking her if her ideas had changed. But I came to see that bisexuality seemed, to Garber and others, to be a necessary replacement for the concept of androgyny. I composed a lengthy letter to Garber, but I never sent it.

Androgyny, I had wanted to tell her, bears no necessary or particular relation to sexual preference. Bisexuality insists, with excellent reason in my view, that without societal and cultural restraints, individuals will be sexually attracted to other individuals, based not on their sex but on the strength of their personal appeal. There is, however, no justification that I can see for supposing that those capable of bisexuality are necessarily androgynous; indeed, many men and women appealing to others of the same sex are overwhelmingly "male" or "female" in appearance and manner. Androgyny, I wanted to tell Garber, is a concept permitting men and women to move, as their inclinations direct them, along the spectrum of "masculine" and "feminine" behavior. Androgyny's aim, as I said all those years ago in the book to which Garber was still so vehemently objecting, is to free individuals from the prison of gender and the dictates of the appropriate.

There has been much talk in recent years of releasing individuals from gender altogether. *The New Yorker,* a weather vane of current topics, had a cartoon in which a parent is saying to a visitor, "We're going to allow the children to pick their gender when they grow up." I have attended symposia where men and women spoke of passing as the other sex, of adopting the "lifestyle" of the other sex. To me, this has always seemed a reinforcement of gender, not a denial of it. Just as transsexuals almost always adopt the most stereotypical behavior of the sex they have transferred to, so transvestites and those playing gender-bending games are still reinforcing the accepted definitions of gender. To masquerade as the other sex is probably great fun; although I have tried to be outrageous in my sixties, I have never undertaken this adventure, never having had a reasonable opportunity, like a dramatic production or a carnival, to induce me to do so. Also, given my figure and voice, I doubt I would be very convincing as a man. But the game of pretending to be the other sex is not androgyny, full of the possibilities of liminality and masquerade as it may be. Androgyny, above all, allows individuals comfort in their own sex, while refusing to recognize the necessity of conforming to constraints dictated by gender.

There is great pleasure in reclaiming in one's sixties an earlier idea one had been persuaded was not altogether acceptable. As I walk comfortably in my ungendered clothes and relish the knowledge that I shall never again have to be uncomfortable through fear of not being legitimate, I have decided that androgyny is an idea whose time has not only come, but will continue to recur as long as women do not choose to have their movements hampered, and do not feel compelled to dress in order to please men and "respectable" women. The need to placate devotees of conformity may, in the wearing of dress and much else, become less imperative as time goes on.

I learned recently that fashion designers who refuse comfort of movement and simplicity of dressing to women go either bankrupt or back to the drawing boards. This is certainly a straw in the wind; it may even be the first sign of an astonishing revolution. Those to whom appearance and desirability are everything will still be able to follow their inclinations: no one here is recommending that we all dress like aging versions of Huckleberry Finn, comfortable as he always seems. But at least some women will wish to be judged by qualities other than their dress, their ability to appear thin and helpless, their success in inspiring male lust.

UNMET FRIENDS

All day I watch for our wild
turkeys, the ones you've tamed
with horse corn, but only the old
one comes, toeing out on his henna feet.
Small-headed, pot bellied, he stands
too tall—I need to think this—
to tempt a raccoon.

—MAXINE KUMIN, "Notes on a Blizzard"

TO FIND UNMET FRIENDS, one must be a reader, and
not an infrequent one. I am always intrigued to hear
from women and men facing retirement that they will
get a chance to read the books they never had time for.
I don't believe this, unless they simply mean read more
steadily, for longer periods. Reading—like those more
frivolous lifelong pursuits, singing in tune, or diving,
or roller-blading—is either an early acquired passion or
not: there is no in-between about it, no catching up in
one's later years. Yet even when men have been lifelong
readers, poring over books at night in bed when life
offered no other suitable periods, they rarely, I suspect,
have unmet friends. Perhaps they move so constantly
in groups that they are seldom lonely and in need of

such companionship. Perhaps no man, reading the life of a contemporary as I have read Maxine Kumin's life, would transform that literary exercise into friendship. Women, I believe, search for fellow beings who have faced similar struggles, conveyed them in ways a reader can transform into her own life, confirmed desires the reader had hardly acknowledged—desires that now seem possible. Women catch courage from the women whose lives and writings they read, and women call the bearer of that courage friend.

Maxine Kumin exists as a close friend only in my mind. Perhaps many writers would like to have their being only in the minds of their readers: represented by their work and otherwise unknown. For me Kumin has been a woman, vital to my sixties, whom I know in a way no biographer or friend can know her: she is her poems and essays, and what I choose to make of them. At its simplest level, she is what I might have wished to become but never could; her life seems to me a very heaven, intermingling animals and poetry.

I came across her many years ago as a poet, before I began to read everything else she had written. She is one of what I fondly call "my" generation of women poets, that is, those who became young adults at the time of World War II and best embody the exciting revelations of feminism, and the sensations of their continuing life as women awakened to much that the world had tried, in their girlhood, to deny them. As with me, Kumin's husband-to-be was in the Navy; her poem about that time might have come from my pen, had I been a poet rather than one devoted to prose almost from the beginning. I suspect that I read poetry so much because, like music, it allows full scope for my listening and reading talents.

We each had two daughters and a son. But what caught me up so absolutely was Kumin's decision, in middle age, to live full-time on her New Hampshire farm, raising and riding horses among many other rural activities. *Harvard Magazine* some years ago published a picture of her in her riding clothes, tall, lean, elegant, standing with a horse. That photograph represented all I could never be, and for many years thought I wanted to be. As Kumin, who has won a Pulitzer prize, wryly puts it: Americans will not pay for poetry, but they will pay you to talk to them about writing poetry. For these talks, she occasionally left her New Hampshire farm and her long-time husband. Her poems are about what she encounters on these trips; about her grown children, miles away; about the losses death has brought. Her total commitment to two lives, poetry and the family farm with horses, entrances me.

May Sarton, to be sure, moved between her flowers and her poetry. But flowers have never tempted me; I enjoy them, but we do not speak, flowers and I. Whether animals admit it or not, they and I communicate. The soft nose of a horse is incitement, though one I have never found a literary use for; except for Kumin's poems and essays, I am sadly horse-deprived. At the same time I know, were I to talk to her of horses, I would sound a fool. Because we have never met, I imagine she always answers me kindly. And instead of boring her with my childlike astonishment at all we have in common, I invent her as a friend.

We might have met at Wellesley College. She applied there, as she reports it, because they had a large swimming pool with an underwater window, and she hoped to be an Olympic swimmer. (Before college, she had sat with her dripping hair at the dinner table, a disappointing daughter, as I, in my saddle shoes instead of ladylike footwear, was a disappointing niece to proper aunts.) Wellesley, with a lack of judgment that seemed to me, then, to mark all their admissions, put her on the waiting list and she went to Radcliffe. (Much later, I came to suspect that her Jewishness did not make her admission likelier). We would have been in the same class, since our birthdays are just a month apart, but would we in reality have become friends? Why am I so sure that we would not? Partly because I, disliking the place and all its ladylike students, was awkward, considered intellectual and probably off-putting (an impression confirmed by my refusal to wear my glasses, without which I could see barely two feet in front of me and recognized no one). We all, even those among us who hated the expected woman's destiny, were female impersonators—a phrase I learned from Gloria Steinem, a mistress of phrases.

Could I, who hated swimming (which was required), have admired a devoted swimmer? Kumin has suggested that she did not begin to question the assumptions about the proper female life until she had children and fell into the misery so prevalent among college-educated women, who ached with discontent and blamed themselves for it: "I began as a poet in the Dark Ages of the fifties, with very little sense of who I was—a wife, a daughter, a mother, a college instructor, a swimmer, a horse lover, a hermit—a stewpot of conflicting emotions."

These were the years, as Kumin describes them, when an editor refused one of her poems because "he had already published a woman in the preceding month." (Steinem, too, met up repeatedly in the sixties with editors who had "already published their woman's piece." Why did that not reverberate with me as did Kumin's experience? I think because Steinem was trying to be a journalist, and I wanted to be, if not a poet—for which I had no gift—at least a writer of books and essays.)

By the time in her life when Kumin found a way to escape being "a stewpot of conflicting emotions," she was writing poetry in the Harvard workshop of John Holmes. (This was a workshop in which Sarton had earlier been a member, to be later forgotten by John Ciardi, who recalled only the male members when he wrote of it. Sarton was used to being wiped out, as though she had never existed, by male poets. Later, Ciardi said that Kumin had a "master's eye.") Kumin had companions in poetry while I was an assistant professor longing for the sort of world Kumin had discovered and of which I would learn only later: a world of martinis, and fellow poet Anne Sexton on the other end of a telephone line:

As the world knows, we were intimate friends and professional allies. Early on in our friendship, indeed almost as soon as we began to share poems, we began to share them on the telephone. Since we lived initially in the same Boston suburb and later in contiguous ones (Ma Bell's unlimited contiguous service be praised!), there were no message units to reckon with. . . . Fairly early on we both installed second phone lines in our houses so that the rest of each of our families—the two husbands, the five children—could have equal access to a phone and we could talk privately for as long as we wanted. I confess we sometimes connected with a phone call and kept that line linked for hours at a stretch, interrupting poem-talk to stir the spaghetti sauce, switch the laundry, or try out a new image on the typewriter; we whistled into the receiver for each other when we were ready to resume. It worked wonders.

Many, thinking of Kumin, think also of Sexton, and the remarkable poems Kumin wrote about her. Pondering Sexton's suicide, Kumin wanted "part of my life back / so I can do it over, / so I can do it better." Her lines haunt me in my sixties: with so many companions lost in the mists of time and busyness, I recall Helen, the friend of my youth, whose husband, I surmised, eventually tiring of the discontent we explored together, told her not to see me anymore. Despite my teaching and writing, I, like Helen, found the undiluted presence of young children alternately frustrating and anxiety producing. She and I talked of what we might do, of what we might write, of how we might place ourselves in the world. And then she was withdrawn from me, as I interpreted it, by a husband certain that a home and children were sufficient for any woman. Some years later, she killed herself. I have always felt that had I not let stand her refusal to see me, not accepted the rejection so easily, I might have prevented her death. For the truth was, I probably provided the only outlet for her in the constant entanglement that Kumin has called "the mothering business." If only I had responded better to her dismissal, refused to be repudiated. But my feelings were hurt, and I let her go her way. Years after, Helen's daughter, looking hauntingly like her, came up to me at a college where I was speaking. I was so overcome that I could scarcely utter a word. Helen did not have time to become accomplished, to even approach the achievements of Sexton, but she was wonderfully gifted, and the wound of her death, and its prelude in her rejection of me, will never heal. But Kumin's poem has given me the words for mourning.

Because of the arrogance and cruelty of male critics, Kumin and Sarton both almost lost for a time their confidence as poets (although Kumin was not ignored by her colleagues in Holmes's workshop, as Sarton had been). When Kumin was at Radcliffe, however, she had shown her poems to an instructor, and, she writes: "Six weeks later he gave them back to me. He had written on the front: 'Say it with flowers, but, for God's sake, don't try to write poems.' That just closed me off; I didn't try to write another poem for about six years." Sarton's *Selected Poems* had fallen for review into the hands of Karl Shapiro, who called her a bad poet. I can testify that she never forgot this cruelty, but at the time, as she puts it, "It took months to recover from the poison."

Even in recent years, I have heard male academics of the more retrograde kind, those who wish to return to the good old days when no one questioned what literature was to be studied, announce that no one reads poetry anymore. If they are on a panel with me, I annoy them by pointing out that women's poetry is widely read, by women and men who are not fearfully guarding their turf. Women's poetry, during the current feminist movement, surged forth with a startling brilliance to the welcome of a wide audience. It troubled some, but intoxicated many more, filling them with a sense of power over their own lives and the circumstances they encountered.

In the new house, my husband and I throw out corn to tempt the wild turkeys, whose discovery of our offering we love to witness. Kumin writes: "All day I watch for our wild / turkeys." But it is not wild turkeys alone, but the fact that we have lived through the same years, chosen and stuck with the same kind of life—heterosexual, long married, children, making it work—that transformed her into my spectral friend. We both remember "The Day / of infamy," as Roosevelt called December 7, 1941, the day the Japanese bombed Pearl Harbor, when we were young girls, "listening to the radio / on a Sunday of hard weather."

Kumin has joined me in my debate with May Sarton over the glories of mothering and families. For many years, I tried to convince Sarton that she idealized these conventional fruits of "womanhood" unreasonably. And then, years later, I came across an interview Kumin had given, in which she was asked to comment on the following statement of Sarton's:

The woman who needs to create works of art is born with a kind of psychic tension in her which drives her unmercifully to find a way to balance, to make herself whole. Every human has the need. In the artist it is mandatory. Unable to fulfill it, he goes mad. But when the artist is a woman she fulfills it at the expense of herself as a woman.

Kumin said: "I'm afraid I don't agree with May Sarton. I don't think that a woman fulfills her need to write at the *expense* of herself as a woman. I think that the creative process is androgynous. It has nothing to do with gender. . . ." To be fair to Sarton, that statement was in a courageous novel, *Mrs. Stevens Hears the Mermaids Singing,* one of the earliest to speak openly of female homosexuality; she may have felt that that statement provided, in those Dark Ages, a certain protection. But it is true that Sarton idealized families, even while clinging to the solitude that made her the ideal and envy of women everywhere, many of them ensconced in families. Kumin, meanwhile, so ensconced, salutes her "androgynous pagan muse," and has written in "Distance":

> Whoever mows with a big machine like this,
> with two forward speeds and a wheel clutch,
>   nippled hand grips,
> a lever to engage the cutting blade, is
>   androgynous
> as is old age, especially for us marathoners.
>
> We are growing into one sex, a little leathery
> but loving, appreciating the air of midday
> embroidered with leaping insects, the glint
>   glancing from
> the flanks of grazing horses, the long
>   puppyhood of the young.

It is, however, in her to me astonishing incarnation as a farm woman and horsewoman, in her passionate maternity, and in her willingness to slave in the kitchen to achieve the fullest possible enjoyment of the fruits of her garden and fields that Kumin exists so vividly for me as an alter ego. As she puts it, she was "programmed into one kind of life, which was to say: get a college degree, get married, and have a family," the same life I, at least superficially, felt myself destined for. The difference began with children: Kumin started, in her words, "to grow up at about age thirty"; her daughters helped. I did not have children till about age thirty, and although my daughters eventually helped me in many ways—for example, to contemplate without terror, as I neared fifty, wearing trousers and flat-heeled shoes—I was already a feminist when they were growing up. Kumin and I resemble each other in that we both began, she as a poet, I as a soon-to-be Ph.D., to find another space beyond "the program" of the 1950s. I accepted the need for total devotion to my children, even if I could not offer them the whole day, every day. We ate together as a family every night, we walked together in the evenings, I cooked every night (thank God before fear-of-cholesterol made daily roasts, alternated with macaroni and cheese, forbidden foods), I worried about my children unceasingly. Between anxiety and guilt—if a child knocked out her teeth in the playground, that was my fault for not being there, wasn't it?—I longed to escape every part of my life that was not family or work, and by work I meant literature, not growing vegetables or raising horses. Kumin lived out the other possible script. She found a way to make mucking out the stalls of horses feed poetry, while I wrote about the possible lives of women and invented a detective who was freer of domestic chores than I could hope for many years to be.

I too was a nature child; I spent two summers in my early teens at ranches, riding horses, caring for them and going on horseback pack trips. But I was also a city child, and in the end, that was the life that called. The summer home we acquired in the fifties was supposed to be what Kumin's turned out to be, but mine never developed into an alternative life. As it failed to provide what it had potentially offered, I came to dislike it, though it took me many years to realize or admit this. I now spend weekends in the small house, eat store-bought food, and, besides the corn for the wild turkeys, provide only a bird feeder to encourage the natural world.

Had Kumin been only a farmer who wrote clever, no matter how clever, essays on her daily struggle with horses, berries, and mushrooms, she would never have had the place she holds in my imagination. It was the poems that made the difference—the poems which combine her country life, a quality of womanhood, and exquisite talent; the poems, natural as speech (requiring great talent), full of pain and the slow wonder of discovery. So she relates how "Nightly I choose to keep this covenant / with a wheezing broodmare . . . ten days past due":

> Sleeping with animals,
> loving my animals too much,
> letting them run like a perfectly detached
> statement by Mozart through all the other lines
> of my life, a handsome family of serene
> horses glistening in their thoughtlessness,
> fear ghosts me still for my two skeletons:
> one stillborn foal eight years ago.
> One, hours old, dead of a broken spine.
> Five others swam like divers into air,
> dropped on clean straw, were whinnied to, tongued
> dry,

and staggered, stagey drunkards, to their feet,
nipped and nudged by their mothers to the teat.

Unlike Steinem, who moved with amazing effec-
tiveness in the public world, or Sarton, who lived
alone and wrote poetry while struggling with rage,
loneliness, and despair, Kumin spanned both the re-
futed and the desired aspects of my life. I needed a
dog to get me out for a walk every morning, but I
would soon have resented horses with their daily demands, and fruits and vegetables with their ulti-
matums of ripeness. The whole idea of woman as
servant, housekeeper, cook, home-manager, stuck in
my throat. I was not, like Kumin, "wretchedly discon-
tented" in the fifties because I had a goal, the Ph.D.,
and a love of literature that perhaps equaled hers of
horses and swimming. To read, to reflect that reading
in prose, were for me sufficient as a life, if barely. She
broke from her wretchedness in one direction, I from
mine in another.

Why do I feel, not having met her but having read
all her work, that she and I are closer in the destinies
we have chosen than I am to many friends personally
known? Here is Kumin, musing (poetically) on her
seventh decade:

Around me old friends (and enemies) are beleaguered
with cancer or clogged arteries. I ought to be
melancholy inching upward through my sixties
surrounded by the ragged edges of so many acres,

parlaying the future with this aerobic mowing,
but I take courage from a big wind staving off the
    deerflies.

Is it because I suspect that had I been wholly successful as a woman I would have been what she is, even
though I despise any definition of successful womanhood? Or is it only that I, like Kumin, have traveled
about, speaking and holding seminars, but that unlike
her I travel without a saddle in my luggage, without a
horse waiting at each destination to provide another
dimension for action, another pace at which to move?
It was only in my sixties that I ceased to long for an
end to my loneliness, that I accepted it as the necessary price for the life I had chosen. Oddly—it is characteristic of the games life plays—once I had accepted
loneliness in my sixties, I found close friends and
refound old friends who, like me, had changed with
life and no longer pursued the old conventional satisfactions. And through Kumin, an exact contemporary
whose path I might many times have crossed, I have
learned that friends unmet can never be lost.

Samuel Johnson commented, in *Rasselas,* upon "the
enduring elegance of female friendship." It is never
wise to take too seriously anything Johnson says about
women, but this phrase, bereft of whatever irony he
intended, perfectly describes the relationship of a
woman reader with a woman writer whose works she
has encompassed, reread, and delighted in. Such

friendships between the woman reader and the author who intrigues her can, like friendships in the flesh, fade or transform themselves into little more than a tender memory, requiring few if any reunions. For many years, Dorothy L. Sayers, creator of Lord Peter Wimsey, was such a writer for me until, one day, my thoughts of her became wispy and perished altogether; I had written about her extensively enough to have diffused what mystery she ever held. Virginia Woolf, on the other hand, a writer I have studied, taught, and written about with admiration, has never been a friend: she is entirely too much of a genius for that. No doubt she would not have liked me had we met (after all, the evidence of her diaries and letters strongly suggests that she did not welcome strangers, least of all Americans), but that is hardly the point. Sayers would not have liked me either (she distrusted Jews and was wary of outspoken feminists), but her life and her writings spoke to me of a more expansive life, an existence devoted to aims riskier than I had previously allowed myself. She, too, therefore, became an unmet friend.

Another is Sylvia Townsend Warner, who confirmed in me my eccentricities, my love of animals, and my devotion (little encouraged these days, but perhaps e-mail will make a difference) to letter writing. Vanessa Bell, who offered an example of devotion to one's art or craft, was also a writer of letters: "Do not snub me with silence," she implored a correspondent. She wished, as she grew older, to be let alone to paint and not induced to accept invitations to social events: "What a blessing it is," she wrote in a letter, "simply to have decided that one won't go to parties. The more I think of it the less reason I see for going. If one has to encounter humans, why not do so in other ways—any way that doesn't entail dressing up. . . . So I sit peacefully at home and write to you."

I have a self-portrait of Vanessa Bell, a somber, self-deprecating but powerful portrait liked by few. Painted when she was nearing fifty, the picture, *Portrait of the Artist,* simultaneously declares her great talent and the diffidence she feels before her concept of the artist she might have been, had she not been a woman doomed to place above all else the welfare of her children and her lovers. At the time we bought the painting, to mark my mother's sudden death twenty years ago, I had short, curly dark brown hair and was hardly a beauty, while Vanessa Bell's beauty was widely celebrated. She had painted herself with glasses, and her hair, pulled back into a bun, was gray. As the years went by, as my hair, now gray and long, was fastened in a bun, I came to look, not like her (that was past praying for) but like her self-portrait. Many visitors assumed it was a portrait I had commissioned of myself: such are the tricks and mockeries of time. Across from Vanessa Bell, in our living room, hangs the self-portrait of her lover and fellow artist, Duncan Grant. He, a man unambiguous in his devotion to art, looks utterly self-confident, unknown to doubt. Over the years, I have derived much wry amusement from this confrontation.

Biographies of women will offer unmet friends provided the subject of the biography has encountered struggles or dilemmas or crises of choice that the reader can learn from, as one would from a friend's. We like, I think, to read as women about women who have braved the terrors and the hopes we share, at least to some degree. Courage in women always catches me up, moves me to compassion and the desire to offer them succor, sustenance if possible. Diana Trilling wrote of Marilyn Monroe's appeal to women, "to whose protectiveness her extreme vulnerability spoke so directly." But, Trilling added sadly, "We were the friends of whom she knew nothing." I was not such a friend. Monroe's life and disasters were so unfamiliar to me, so beyond even my sympathetic imagining, that I could not be an unmet friend to her. The secret to unmet friends is that they have called upon the same strengths to escape or endure the same kinds of situations.

Oddly enough, even to women who are fond of, even extravagantly devoted to, men, the lives and fictions of men do not serve in the same way. I have pondered this long and hard. The answer, I think, is that men have it too easy just from having been born male. Example: The men I was friends with in graduate school in the fifties—*the* fifties, not my fifties—

remember me as having fun, full of talk and excitement, enjoying myself, as they were. They are right, but they could not know then the anxieties I hid, as a mother, as a woman fearing to be thought too bold, fearing worse to be timid and obsequious and to lose myself. They could not know the guilt I felt as the companion of men who had wives at home to watch the children, do the laundry, and know themselves unable to talk shop with their husbands as I could. The slights that Sarton and Kumin had to bear, as poets, from men were not slights any man, however wonderful, could know. (I must add, however, that some of these men, and their wives, have come a long, long way and understand a good deal now.) But even now, men and women cannot experience life's agonies in the same way. Men complain, but not of the same things that harry women. So Sylvia Townsend Warner implored Marchette Chute: "*Please* don't write a life of Milton. It is such a melancholy subject, the way the English Angel, flourishing about in Italy, degenerated into a public figure, generally cross about something. There is quite enough to depress one as it is, without being reminded of Milton."

Unmet friendships, whether sustained in letters or by one individual's solitary reading of another's work, have a lasting quality, able to endure all changes, all possible calamities. As Sylvia Townsend Warner's biographer said of her, "She loved, and needed, the uncluttered intellectual intimacy" which correspondence allowed. Warner herself, in her biography of T. H.

White, defined "a correspondence kept up over a length of years with never a meeting" as a "bridge." But, she continued, "It is a bridge that only carries the weight of one person at a time. When the correspondents meet it collapses and they have to founder their way to the footing of actuality."

Unmet friends never test the bridge of their one-way correspondence. And if, like Kumin, such a friend writes essays and poems, the bridge from her to her reader can never collapse as long as the reader lives.

LISTENING
TO THE YOUNG(ER)

"You are old," said the youth, "one would hardly suppose
    That your eye was as steady as ever;
Yet you balanced an eel on the end of your nose—
    What made you so awfully clever?"

"I have answered three questions, and that is enough,"
    Said his father. "Don't give yourself airs!
Do you think I can listen all day to such stuff?
    Be off, or I'll kick you down-stairs!"

LEWIS CARROLL, Alice's Adventures in Wonderland

FATHER WILLIAM WAS RIGHT: if the young are asking too many questions, there's an unexpressed motive somewhere. They sometimes want to console the rapidly aging, but when the young ask for advice or information they are playing either the sycophant or an assigned role in a script designed by someone else. Carroll's poem is a parody of what Martin Gardner, an annotator of the Alice books, calls "a long-forgotten didactic poem by Robert Southey," very famous in its day. In the Southey poem, Father William uses the youth's questions to give good advice, telling the young man to behave properly and to remember that "the pleasures of youth pass away." In Cicero's *De Senectute,* the young men stand around (I imagine them shifting from foot to foot) while they listen to Cicero's arguments about the glories of old age; they, too, are props giving excuse for Cicero's fulminations: what he says is wise, but the young will never believe it. There are few old people who have not wished to tie a young person down, hand and foot, and tell her or him the truth about life. Unfortunately, the young person will not listen, and the old person will inevitably come across as, at best, a tedious bore.

Lewis Carroll understood the practicality, not to mention the monotony, of sanctimonious answers, and therefore makes fun of the questions and ends by having Father William refuse to answer another. When Alice, told by the Caterpillar to recite the Southey poem, comes up with the parody, the Caterpillar is irritated:

"That is not said right," he announces.

"Not *quite* right, I'm afraid," says Alice timidly.

"It is wrong from beginning to end," the Caterpillar decidedly says.

But of course the poem is right, particularly at its end. Should the young ask for advice they are up to no good, and kicking them downstairs should be offered in response to such a pretense; three questions is more than enough of *that.*

The young, of course, assume—due, I fear, to the unfortunate inclinations of some of us in our later years—that we are dying to tell them endlessly about our experiences, and about the light these experiences throw on the mistakes customary to youth, and particularly in the youth we are addressing. The secret, however, of successful—and therefore continuing—association with the young lies in knowing that they are more valuable as suppliers of intelligence than receivers of it. Nor is getting them to inform us a difficult task. As Marilyn French described it in *My Summer with George,*

one really charming quality of the narcissistic younger generation is their distractibility; you can easily deflect any unwanted attention they may direct at you simply by asking them about themselves.

Although the old, as we are daily warned, are growing in numbers while the population of the young yearly declines, it is the young who influence the world we live in. Everyone from actors to tennis players to writers is getting younger. Except in advertisements of dentifrices designed for the wearers of false teeth or laxatives to rescue the aging from their constipation, the young dominate the airwaves, television, the fashion ads, the Internet (and the technology to access it), and the movies. The aging, while nervous about HMOs, Medicare, and Social Security, do not seem to play a very large role in this country's affairs—aging women even less than men. If, therefore, we wish to keep up with at least some part of what is going in the world, it is the young to whom we must turn.

Without my children, my graduate students, and my friends ten years younger than I and counting, I would be probably be living in a state of sad self-satisfaction, ignorant of much that is happening around me. Not about politics, which one can follow readily enough, or events, like O. J. Simpson's trial, screaming at us from every corner, but the feel of life, its beat as it sounds each day. Lionel Trilling, speaking of what he called "manners," put this so well that I must let him say it for me:

What I understand by manners is a culture's hum and buzz of implication. I mean the whole evanescent context in which its explicit statements are made. It is that part of a culture which is made up of half-uttered or unuttered or unutterable expressions of value. They are hinted at by small actions, sometimes by . . . tone, gesture, emphasis, or rhythm, sometimes by the words that are used with a special frequency or a special meaning.

It is precisely this that we ought to pick up from the young. To try and stay sufficiently *au courant* to know it all ourselves is difficult, tedious, and affected. Our deepest feelings are, I think, in a different place. But to cut the hum and buzz completely from our consciousness, dismissing it with a tired or, worse, critical gesture, is to cut ourselves off from our culture and the delightful sense of, however superficially, learning something new while regarding it with that peaceful (but never complacent) distance age provides.

The lives of the young tend to be tumultuous and thus offer us, if we have young friends, vicarious experience of the best kind, the kind it would be painful in the extreme, not to say ludicrous, to have to undergo oneself. Friendships between those of sufficiently different generations, so that the variance in years counts for markedly distinct experiences, offer satisfying knowledge and vicarious experience to the old. In the history of their sex lives, if in no other way, the young and I, I am delighted to discover, might have belonged to cultures many miles and many centuries apart. My day-to-day experiences are, on the whole, and barring disasters, predictable; without hearing from the young, I would feel only half alive.

Most of my young friends are smarter than I am. They sometimes argue with me about this, which is kind of them and I appreciate it, but the young being smarter—which is not to say wiser—is the whole point. One of the dangers inherent in friendships among the old is that they are no smarter now than they ever were; one usually knows them all too well, and vice versa. In Virginia Woolf's *To the Lighthouse*, Mr. Bankes, regretting what has become of his relationship to Mr. Ramsay, thinks: "What with one thing and another, the pulp had gone out of their friendship. Whose fault it was he could not say, only, after a time, repetition had taken the place of newness.

It was to repeat that they met." With those who are younger, one is much less likely to repeat.

An older woman has told me a story about my lawyer son when he was in law school that nicely demonstrates how the young may serve those further along in life. This older woman entered law school when she was past fifty and when her youngest child was in college, becoming my son's classmate. The work did not faze her, but long-entrenched guilt toward her children did, as it does most mothers. At the end of the first term, her child in college called to say: "But who will make the Christmas cookies?" Since my son, who is large, had raised her, who is small, over his head in celebration of her winning the moot court competition, she went to him for consolation over this complaint. My son looked at her: "Fuck the Christmas cookies," he pronounced. She told me this years later, filling my reluctant maternal heart with feminist pride, as hers had, for a single moment, overflowed with relief.

So if those who are younger talk, and those who are older listen, and if, as I believe, the young like to talk to or anyway "at" those older, for the very same satisfaction the difference in generations offers each, isn't it pretty much a one-way street? Do we who are getting on serve only to listen to the young? Have we nothing to tell them that is worth their hearing, even if they may feel a little bored hearing it? I do not mean that we sit silent and judgmental, like doctrinaire Freudian analysts; we speak, we respond, we question.

But as I pondered this a good while I came only recently to understand that it is our very presence that is important to the young. They want us to be there: not in their homes, perhaps, not watching them with a baleful eye as they go about their daily work, but *there*. We reassure them that life continues, and if we listen, we assure them that it matters to us that it continues. If we do not tiresomely insist that the past was better, that the present is without morals or good habits or healthy living or (heaven help us) family values, whatever they are; if we do not insist on recounting ancient anecdotes as original as a tape recording and as easily rendered audible; if we do not recount adventures in the past, even if requested to do so, then the young will sometimes actually seek—they will not openly ask—for something we are equipped to give them. What to call it? It is the essence of having lived long, it is the unstated assurance that most disasters pass, it is the survival of deprivation and death and rejection that renders our sympathy of value.

I can remember graduating from college and assuring myself that never, never would I look like those old fragile beings staggering along in the academic procession. Perhaps the young can sense what I now know: that I may look like some of those ancient beings, but inside of me I can still partake of all the spontaneous joy of youth—to which is added the exquisite unlikelihood of its recurrence. Like lovers parting in wartime, who may never meet again or know each other if they do, we who grow old can taste the biting edge of passion's anticipated annulment, and savor it as the young cannot. But I believe the young perceive what we cannot tell them.

LIVING WITH MEN

Husband. A repressive word, that, when you come to think of it, is compounded of a grumble and a thump.

DOROTHY L. SAYERS, Busman's Honeymoon

IN ONE'S SIXTIES, no less than in the years preceding them, even the most male-centered woman can find men becoming the object of despair and hatred. Momentary hatred. Feminists are often accused of being man-haters, which is untrue. I know no feminist who hates men; I don't even know any lesbians who hate men. Many women bear something akin to hatred for the patriarchy—the system that puts men and their requirements at the center of every orbit—but individual men (many of whom share women's suspicions of this arrangement) are no more the object of that antipathy than individual Southerners are the object of acrimony toward slavery. Loathing Rush Limbaugh and Pat Robertson does not imply a hatred of "men," not least because some of the most persistent antifeminists are women. I'm sure that point is perfectly clear.

Having made it, I shall proceed to the declaration that no woman has failed to reverberate, late or soon, often or seldom, to the conviction that men are outrageous monsters of insensitivity who probably should be shunned for life if we could only figure out any way to do without them. Even if as women we love other women and live with them as partners, we are still likely to be possessed of fathers, brothers, sons, and even possibly, at some dim point in our history, a male lover or a husband. And no one who has spent any time at all with a male can fail to consider them, on occasion, impossible.

Doris Lessing has wondered if anyone observing humankind might not conclude that men and women were different species, so diverse are their habits, obsessions, and pastimes. It is an idea that has occurred to all women at one time or another. My own conclusion, reached at this late date, is that men and women who meet upon occasion, whether for conversation, sex, companionship, or mild flirtation of the sort that used to be encompassed in the now outworn phrase *amitié amoureuse,* tend to find each other more companionable than men and women who live together, day in, day out, sharing real estate, groceries, the care of a child, and intrusions upon what could happily be solitary time. I have no doubt this is why extramarital affairs are so much more satisfying, at least temporarily, than plain old matrimony, even if either partner would not dream of changing her or his mate for an afternoon lover.

The reason before all other reasons intermittent dalliances are so satisfying is that occasional male companions and lovers *listen*—that rare quality which seems to appear in males only for an hour a day at the outside, or when lust is aroused. Men are not listeners, and I have not the slightest doubt that psychoanalysis got off to such a sticky clinical start because Freud and Breuer, and all men like them, are really lousy listeners. They hear what they expect to hear, or want to hear, or are certain they will hear, and women, being supple creatures trained to please, have often told them what we women knew would satisfy them.

Many women have found erotic the fact that a strange man "sees" them. Most males, as is well known, do not *see* the women they regularly encounter. Jokes have long been made about men who admire a new hat that their wife has owned for three seasons, but it can be more serious than that. James Watson, he who chased after and triumphantly seized the Nobel prize for describing DNA (this is an approximation of his accomplishment) gave little credit to his female collaborator, Rosalind Franklin, and, adding insult to injury, sneered at her because, among other reasons, she wore glasses. Rosalind Franklin never wore glasses, but Watson apparently assumed that a brainy woman in danger of winning some of the praise so obviously due him must have been bespectacled; didn't all brainy, impossible women wear glasses? (Anne Sayre, who wrote *Rosalind Franklin and DNA,* had been Franklin's friend and came to doubt Watson's account of her contribution to his work when she read his description of Franklin wearing glasses.)

Franklin died of cancer at thirty-eight and thus could not defend herself.

Men do not listen or see very well beyond their already programmed expectations, and—as any wife will tell you—they do not remember very well either. A woman finds herself making the same request about some domestic matter over and over again, only to be ignored or informed that the whole subject is unworthy of her time, meaning his. I recall, from my youthful readings of J. P. Marquand's novels, a moment in *The Late George Apley* when his wife says to him (this is an approximation) "Do you love me, George?" and he says "of course," and she says "George, please don't say 'of course' anymore, will you try?" and George, of course, says "of course."

Men are bossy; they can't help themselves, and while the training in brutality learned at Virginia Military Institute was praised as divinely suited to form "men," this brings into question the definition of "men." Has it occurred to no one to wonder if men ought not also to learn how *not* to be bossy? Now that the Supreme Court (all but Justice Antonin Scalia) has voted to let women, too, partake of VMI's valuable training, perhaps some question about this may filter through from one sex to the other.

It isn't that women aren't also bossy: they often are. "Harry, I've asked you a hundred times not to leave your shoes in the hall where everyone will trip over them in the dark." But men will say, if you both are gardening, perhaps: "Don't put the whatevers that close together, or that far apart, or that deep or that shallow." *They* know how something *should* be done, whereas in their eyes female knowledge is not knowledge at all, but merely an attitude designed to interfere with male comfort. Gloria Steinem had a story about this. In urging her audience to do one outrageous act a day, and agreeing to do one herself as part of the bargain, she suggested, as an outrageous act, that women might say to the man they live with, "Pick it up yourself." A woman in the audience responded that that was all very fine, but how did you *make* him pick it up? A small, elderly lady in the rear of the large hall managed to get Steinem's attention. "Yes," Steinem said encouragingly. "I nail his underwear to the floor," the elderly lady said. Good advice. "And," another woman added, "don't worry woman-like about your 'nice' floor. Nail as long as you need to and then get the floor done over."

I have long noticed that men will rarely accept logic from a woman, certainly not if they're married to her. Example: We garage our car, and the garages in our neighborhood move around or change owners or close down for a while, and, what with one thing or another, the names of our garages keep changing. My husband always lists them in his telephone book under their name of the moment. Of course he forgets it from time to time, but I don't mention this; men have odd egos and don't care to be reminded of their consistent failings. What I do suggest is that instead of listing the garages by name, he list them, as I do in my phone book, under *g* for *garage,* so that you don't have to remember any given name. This is a hint I picked up years ago from my mother, who listed the telephone numbers of all my acquaintances under *c* for *Carol's friends.* My husband will have none of it.

I read from time to time well-funded studies demonstrating that men are more violent than women, are more aggressive, take more pleasure in causing pain, enjoy killing helpless animals, and are incapable of asking for directions when lost. These characteristics, while no doubt sadly accurate at least where armies are concerned, have not been borne out (except among male adolescents, where they all apply) by my admittedly meager and protected experience of men—a handful of male friends, a husband, a son, a son-in-law, and a grandson who seems, at under a year, boisterous, careless of his own safety, but not in any way mean. No, from my experience and that of such women as I have consulted, there are only two constant factors always present in the male personality. One is an unwillingness, an absolute refusal, to admit that they have an unconscious, that any of their speech or actions could be caused by unconscious impulses or wishes. They may have discovered or had discovered for them the root in childhood of some of their actions, but that interpretation is no longer unconscious. Second is a total inability to change any part of themselves but their appearance even if they proclaim a desire to change.

Women, on the other hand, are always undergoing

change, sculpting and resculpting their personalities and characters as though these were so much clay. But we do not seem to learn that pleading "Couldn't you not contradict me when I speak about money?" or "Couldn't you tuck your tie in and not drop food all over it?" is all in vain. The fundamental disparity between men and women, the reason for their seeming to belong to different species or at best to provide an example of extreme dimorphism, is that women are always trying to change without men's noticing that they are trying, and women are always asking men to change with no evident result. This sort of thing can lead to a certain amount of weary tolerance and despair, but who notices? Not men, for sure. Female behavior is shrugged off as a part of nature, like gravity.

Any woman who has lived with a man over a period of time will tell you that men have cycles just as women do. They do not, however, like women, have any physical evidence for women to point to, and the fact that every man can be expected to become irritable and in some cases irrational once a month has never entered the scientific literature, most of it written by men. Women have menopause and men have midlife crises: nomenclature is all. Women are supposed to be moody, but men are moodier by far in the usual course of things.

I find myself putting all this down now that I am seventy because I more or less figured it all out in my sixties. I don't know whether it was that women started complaining more frequently and insistently to me about men when I was in my sixties, or whether I just began noticing how irrational the "rational" sex is, but I think this revelation is mostly due to my not caring anymore what most men think. I started to stop caring once I had turned fifty, but it took me into my sixties to get this new faculty under my belt. Feminism, and the recognition that the personal reflects the political, had long affected my views on relations between the sexes. But for some reason the revelation that all the troubles women found themselves in with regard to men were part of the general tendencies of men everywhere, and in all cultures had escaped me until now. Girls, certainly girls in my young days and, I suspect, many girls now, are brought up to believe that if you are nice "they" will love you. One goes to work and it is all too long before one realizes—well, it was pretty long before I realized—that if you aren't doing what they want, they aren't going to love you no matter how nice you are. And so in my sixties I realized that I might just as well admit that pleasing oneself is the best way: suit yourself—then at least one person will be happy. This was how the mother of the great dialect scholar and feminist, Joseph Wright, put it; she was a woman Virginia Woolf liked to quote, no doubt considering her responsible for her feminist son.

Oddly enough, deciding that my husband, like all men, has his male characteristics—which mostly manifest themselves as refusal to look within, to change, or to consider me to be, most of the time, a rational being—has made me even fonder of him. Well, that's just his way, I think, as though he were, as he is, an old friend whose peculiarities have ceased to be annoying and become even endearing, now that I know nothing will ever change.

People are often asking me, since I have been married a very long time, the secret of an extended, mostly satisfying marriage. I don't really know how to answer them, but the truth is, at least on my part, that I have come to accept the fact that if one is married to a man, this is what is to be expected on the debit side, just as, if you have a cat as a pet, you expect the furniture to get clawed. I know you can declaw cats, and perhaps husbands too, but I don't approve of it in either case. If an animal is designed by nature to have claws it ought to keep them, and if men come with quirks that they are incapable of changing, well, a certain amount of quietude and even peace can be achieved by just realizing that it's all inherent in the beast.

There is another insight about men that has recently dawned upon me. I mentioned it only the other day to a man with whom I shared a mutual woman friend, now dead. We both commented on the amazing vitality and decisiveness of our friend, and the quiet, almost self-effacing manner of her husband. The husband, as we both knew, was a highly intelligent, brave man, but he seemed almost invisible and was certainly inaudible in her presence.

I offered him on the spot the explanation I had just then formulated about certain marriages: that men, particularly those disinclined—by training, early experience, or birth—to express emotion, will marry a woman capable of strong emotion and powerfully disposed to express it. Is it not possible, I asked this friend, that some men compensate for their lack of emotion by marrying a woman who will provide it for them—become angry for them, excited for them, intense for them? Whether they make their choice of wife consciously or not, their need to have emotion readily available on a daily basis is profound, and the marriage, though comical to outsiders, is in fact deeply satisfactory to both their needs. For of course the wife's need to be passionately expressive in such a marriage is equal to the husband's need for her passion.

In the old days—that is, when I was young—such marriages were the butt of every comic and every psychologist. The man was called henpecked, the woman a harpy, and if they had a son who turned out to be gay, the fault was assumed to be the result of this gender imbalance. All this was nonsense, as were so many gender theories in my youth. Just as some women could not easily endure without male composure and competence in certain mechanical and computer areas, so there are men who would perish for lack of emotional expression without a wife to offer it in their stead. That, at least, is my latest analysis of some not uncommon marriages. "You ought to write a book about that," my friend said as I took my leave. Not a book, perhaps, but it seems a thought worth a paragraph or two to explain some men in some marriages.

I recognize, I assure you, the irony of speaking about "all" men when the major thrust of feminism has been to avoid statements about "all" women, and when nothing arouses most females to fury (even when sung by Bob Dylan) more than being told that she has behaved "just like a woman." The only possible defense I can offer is that the patriarchy, millenniums old, has endowed males with a sense of entitlement, of being the preferred sex, of having been promised at birth opportunities for dominance, aggression, and patronage, which they are able to change, even as individuals, far more slowly than those who have never been at the top of every known social hierarchy. As long as we live in a world where, in India, Africa, China, and the Middle East especially, only boys are prized, and girls are in some places even abandoned or aborted simply because of their sex, men will remain inclined to demonstrate the attributes of this dominance, this preference. And so it will probably continue until sex and gender are matters of almost entire indifference.

Meanwhile, we women live with men, often need them precisely because they are the preferred sex, and can manage current arrangements between the sexes more happily if our anger is generally directed at "all men," rather than particularly aimed at the representative males who shares our lives. The aim of feminism, of course, is not alone to permit women all the various roles hitherto reserved for men, but also to initiate men into the roles hitherto assigned to women. I doubt that even my granddaughter, born toward the end of my sixties, will see so profound a change as that by the end of her sixties. But here's hoping.

SADNESS

In sooth, I know not why I am so sad;
It wearies me; you say it wearies you;
But how I caught it, found it, or came by it,
What stuff 'tis made of, whereof it is born
I am to learn;
And such a want-wit sadness makes of me,
That I have much ado to know myself.

—SHAKESPEARE, *The Merchant of Venice*

I CAN REMEMBER quoting these lines in a letter to my father while I was at Wellesley. It was not a complaint I meant to convey; my father considered me to be unbelievably privileged to have, in contrast to the hard struggle of his youth, four years in so beautiful a college, and I could hardly tell him how miserable I was in that place. No, it was a certain melancholy I wrote of, one that no counting of my blessings (a cure frequently suggested by him then and in subsequent years) served to banish. Indeed, it is in part one's blessed state that allows the sadness to emerge, and to be edged with, not exactly guilt, but a conscience of mild disgrace.

Sadness such as mine is not depression; it can be

blown away by an interesting conversation, a welcome telephone call, or a compelling idea for an essay or piece of fiction. It returns without evident cause, however obvious the cause of its banishment, and it belongs, I have come to suspect, to both youth and age, less frequently to the years between.

When my children were young, when I was working, almost always tired, deprived both of sleep and privacy, I could be beset by irritation, gloom, self-pity, and, occasionally, despair or what I chose to call despair. What I define as sadness, what I think Antonio, in the above quotation, defined as sadness, is a more mysterious affliction, and it returns to me from time to time in these final decades of life.

There is a certain pleasure in this sadness, arising in large part from the inexplicableness of its onset. Rather as one can with certain kinds of flu or head cold lie in bed, slightly feverish, definitely miserable, yet peaceful in one's inactivity, in one's passive repose, so I succumb to sadness. One has, at least for the nonce, given up. One is, meanwhile, sustained by the knowledge that this state will pass, activity will return.

Such an analogy is, of course, limited. Sadness, unlike minor illness, carries with it the shadow of all that has troubled human beings and, most particularly these days, what afflicts those in pain, troubled relationships, or poverty. Yet, at the same time, sadness is the mark of those who bear none of these afflictions, which is why Antonio and I cannot account for it in any decisive manner. It gathers, like a fog, when there is no crisis or explicit basis for fear or desperation, no craving to be healed.

The antithetical or perhaps mirror image to sadness is the experience, similarly unique to one's late years, of a swift, mysterious wave of happiness, also causeless, but of much shorter duration. I cannot remember a time, before my sixties, when the consciousness of happiness would sweep over me and, like a shower of cold water when one is desperately overheated, offer me a passing sensation very close to glee.

Both sadness and fleeting happiness relate, I think, to mortality, to the consciousness of being old and of nearing the end of life. Not that I, for one, consider death, which will be reached, or the aching beauty of nature, which will be lost, in connection with either of these sensations, which surge up from the unconscious, to be a gift of long life or fortunate old age. Both sadness and happiness, but sadness more, are related to the fact that nothing of all this will endure for long. How often I have heard a contemporary or person older than I exclaim with relief, "At least I won't live to see *that*!" whatever *that* is: the destruction of the natural world, the end of reading or of classical music as popular forms, the cheapening effects of television, the spread of terrorism, the effects of the cruel arrogance of those who would deprive others of society's benefits.

My sixties covered a period of pronounced meanness in the United States and in the world, meanness arising from a sense of righteousness and the need to punish, preferably with violence, those who do not share one's beliefs. For the first time in my life, I became fearful of institutionalized religion, which I had never honored but never feared. Now I perceived institutionalized religion as defined chiefly or only by its enemies: groups who did not live lives considered virtuous by those more narrow in their ancient creeds were to be terrorized, violated, and condemned as insufficiently obedient to God. I became awakened, sadly, to policies determined to transpose the symptoms of our societal failures into its causes: the poor, that is, were to be blamed for the failures of a mean-spirited nation that condemned them to poverty.

What might be called political sadness arises, I have found, not from a single affront, or even a multiplicity of them, but as an indirect response to organized and publicly condoned selfishness and revenge about which it seems one can do little or nothing. Contributions to those seeking to ameliorate injustice do not mitigate the weight of this sadness. I am not a person of faith, but I do ponder the extensive and timeless betrayal by religious fanatics of the teachers in whose name these fanatics claim to act. My friend Tom Driver, minister and professor at Union Theological Seminary, dedicated his book *Christ in a Changing World* "to all who have suffered at the hands of people who claimed to act in the name of Christ." This dedication reflects a sadness which he and I, as longtime friends, share.

I have spoken little here of how politics and violence have concerned me in the late years of my life, but I have no doubt that the constant pelting of my consciousness by institutionalized arrogance, revenge, intolerance, and unkindness has often reduced me to a sense of helplessness which leads, in turn, to sadness. I follow the news in *The New York Times* and on National Public Radio, but not on television; I detest sound bites, the banishment of complexity, and, above all, the frequent hammering of commercials.

Daily anger is a different matter, aroused by the "insolence of office," the arrogance of those "dressed in a little brief authority," as Hamlet enumerated these indignities, or by "greetings where no kindness is," as Wordsworth put it, and it is not, I believe, a condition special to one's last years. It is rather the prevailing climate in which we all live. That anger I try, now, to displace with what equanimity I can summon, a difficult task. But one of the benefits of these years is a long backward view, replete with cycles; this helps to calm me. And, as a teacher of modernism, I am aware how tumultuous the last years of the nineteenth century were, and how much that is valuable now emerged from the chaos of those years.

Looking backward, of course, produces another sadness in old age: inevitably one recalls sweeter times, or times that seemed more innocent, less grasping and destructive. All old people have ever been prone to this, and even while I remind myself how fatuous are such theories of deterioration, I remember the greater spread of country in my youth. My father and I would sometimes drive from New York City without special aim, continuing until we had seen a cow. The drives were never long; neither the suburbs nor real estate developments had yet claimed all the fields and farms within an hour of New York. Life seemed simpler because I was young and simple. Yet on the nearest shopping avenue to where I grew up there were small shops, butchers, shoemakers, barbers, mom-and-pop groceries, and not the endless repetition of clothing chains that have now pushed all these individual enterprises out. When I was young there was no overnight parking in the streets, no fights, sometimes to the death, for legal parking spaces, no traffic jams or gridlock.

I know this sort of thing to be foolishness even as, sometimes sadly, I dwell on it. If, looking back, I remember more space, more quiet, more contemplation, if I recall that educated people wrote English, not theoretical jargon, that no one used words like *catachresis* or *aporia,* if I recall all this with passing sadness, I remind myself that when I was a girl, women's lives were restricted in ways all unknown to the young today, while Negroes, as they were called, were segregated and denied the rights of citizenship. I remind myself of Sherlock Holmes saying to Watson that more crime is committed in lonely, isolated rural dwellings than in London. What we think of as idyllic only looks that way to sightseers from other places, and other times.

True sadness which is not nostalgia can, I have

found, be dispelled by reading: by that same literature which seemed, in my youth, to hold both excitement, wisdom, and all I could discover of truth; and by today's newly perceptive books. Lifelong readers continue to read, finding in books, as Samuel Johnson said, the means to enjoy life or to endure it. My reading diet is varied, and changes according to my mood or expectations. I can vividly recall reading in snatches when my children were young, reading with delicious guilt when I should have been preparing classes or doing research, falling asleep over books which were nonetheless enthralling, and these recollections add definite spice and delectability to my reading now, and revive me when I am sad.

Since my retirement, I have lost my taste for literary criticism, not only because of its turgid vocabulary but because it seems, now, so distant from the works it pretends to illuminate. Even feminist criticism, which I used to cherish and celebrate, has become dull to me, often twisting in upon itself, mindless of the passion that infused early publications in this mode. Yet even as I write this, I detest my resemblance to those who still wish to go on teaching in the old way, reading the same books, asking the same questions; I feel ashamed. The shame of old age is in sounding petulant about the young and those who ask unfamiliar questions. Those gentler times to which we old hark back imprisoned and excluded too many of us. Still, in reading, weary now of smartness and glib advice or analysis, I read biography and fiction. I remain incurably Anglophile, readier to read biographies of Philip Larkin, Angus Wilson, Elizabeth Bowen, and Virginia Woolf than equally qualified biographies about Americans; my whole reading life has been and still is primarily English. I have, for example, from her essays and from literary gossip, the distinct impression that should A. S. Byatt and I meet, we would probably disagree on many points. Yet I find her novels, with their immense and varied information and their incisive characterization, a remarkably good antidote to sadness, especially as I imbibe her extensive knowledge of insects and snails. Byatt, and many of her fellow English novelists, can be counted on to perk me up.

Sadness ultimately resides in the knowledge that all *this,* all I look upon, will continue unchanged when I am no longer here to see it. Oddly, I think of it in those terms, rather than simply regretting my absence from these scenes. I suspect this is characteristic of sadness in the last years. The idea of death, of one's disappearance from the stage, evokes the regret that these eyes, this appreciation, this particular apperception, will be gone from the world, not that *I* will not be here. Perhaps this seems hardly a distinction, more a matter of splitting hairs: perhaps it is. But will anyone again look at *that* tree, read *that* poem, love a dog in quite my way? I am a particular and, despite the commonness of all people, a unique person in the way I perceive and think and appreciate, and I am sad that this particularity shall before too long be gone. This is not arrogance; it is the simple truth, known to anyone who has loved a person dead in the fullness of her life: what we miss is that particularity, that unique voice.

When I am sad, I regret that my adult children will no longer hear my voice, nor I theirs. Throughout most of history, mothers hardly lived to see their children become mature adults; novels, like life, concluded more often than not with the consolation of seeing them married. If I do not delude myself about my children's need for me in the years of their middle-age, I am nonetheless sad knowing, as I believe all parents living past their sixties know, that I possess insights that will not endure without me, discernments that will not again find exactly the same expression.

Today women live long into their children's adult lives, and while much has been made recently of the burden such parents are to these middle-aged children, who are also responsible for their own families, too little is made of the pleasure we women feel in conversing with our grown children, and in allowing ourselves, from time to time, to think of them as friends. I have been fortunate in having children with whom conversation is possible; the sheerest pleasure here, for me, has been in meeting with each of them alone, just the two of us, relating to each other what May Sarton, quoting a Spanish proverb, used to call our life and miracles. I now almost always find the opinions of my children perceptive, even if I disagree, and frequently more informed than my own interpretations. When it comes to popular culture, they are, in my total ignorance, a necessary, frequently consulted, resource.

As a teacher in graduate school I have been granted the pleasure of getting to know young adults and learning from them their new views of literature, their easy familiarity with modern theories and computers, their knowledge of foreign countries, not only European ones, and their incisive expression of their own generation's sins and virtues, often so mysterious to me and my colleagues. With my own children it is both easier and harder. It is easier because we share so much, little need be spelled out; we speak, as they say, the same language. (Or perhaps I mean that when they are with me they speak my language, one that was for a long time theirs; there is the ease of recurring gestures, body language, old intimate reassurances that can be counted on.) It is harder because of the emotional weight I carry as a parent, the burdens accumulated through the years of their infancy, childhood, and youth. There are things a parent must never say, simple phrases or observations which can cause violent outrage in a matter of seconds. One learns to skate around these, to avoid them, eventually to forget them.

There is one old lady whom I have known all my life and visit to this day; every time I see her she has some deleterious comment to make about my clothes or hair. I expect this, it comes, and much of the affection I have worked up for her since the last time we met is smothered by her acerbic comment and the resentment it evokes. Talking to adult children entails, I have learned, the avoidance of any comment, however innocuous it may seem, with long trails of emotion and repeated indignation attached. If the relationship is truly a friendly one, new comments and questions, even of a vaguely critical nature, may sometimes be permitted, but only rarely. Perhaps it is the same with all friendships and affections that are both long-lasting and constantly renewed, but with adult children, as any parent whose children are pleasingly attentive can tell you, a special gift of conversation must be learned. I suspect that the children have also discovered this, although the occasional remark about some aspect of their childhood that still does not meet with their approval may surface now and then and must be assiduously ignored, dismissed with a shrug. All children will eventually consider themselves able to be better parents than their parents were. And so they should.

I find myself reflecting that I shall miss them, all three, all differently when I am dead—even as I recognize this to be sentimental nonsense. What I mean is that I hope they will miss me, and such a hope inevitably contains a melancholy element. My casual talk with my adult children brings with it another fleeting sadness: They are the age I was when it became, because of profound political differences, difficult for me to chat easily with my parents: vituperation always lurked. They and I were later reconciled, but those years of loss now add a special poignancy.

Now that I have lived almost as many years as had my parents when the violence and controversy over the Vietnam war divided us, I realize what is obvious but what I never before faced so starkly: As we age, gathering decades on our own account, and if our parents have not died young, we inevitably discover that we lived part of our lives in a world in which our parents never really joined us. I know now that half my life is still loitering where my parents lived; I honor and perhaps in part envy what I still manage to perceive as the coherent simplicity of that universe. The other half, the part that moved me away from my origins, contemplates a world my parents never knew, a world they could hardly understand or sympathize with except by gigantic effort.

The poignancy I feel because of the years my parents and I lost through sharp political deviation has, I now suspect, a general rather than a special pathos. When our parents die, and especially if they do not, as mine did not, undergo long, hard deaths but leave life still engaged with it, we see our parents whole for the first time. They no longer change as our view of them changes because we change; they preserve the unity of personality we grant our contemporaries. Yet whether we feel admiring of our parents, reconciled to them, or still estranged, still teetering near a cliff of anger, we recognize that we can never meet them in agreement about what we have encountered beyond their experience.

I know that is how it will be for my children when I am dead. I know that however attentively I listen to them now as they recount the strange details of the culture they take for granted and I observe from an admiring or bewildered distance, my life when I am dead will become whole in their eyes, but nonetheless divided between their world and mine. It may be that this is one reason the young do not want to hear about our past, about how it was when we were their age. They may sense that one day they too will cease to live completely in the present that surrounds them, not because they remember their past or pay it much attention, but because inevitably their children, or the young people they know, will assign them, as they will assign themselves, to a different, largely abandoned world.

This thought can, in certain moods, promote sadness. But its inevitability, at least for me, quickly defeats that sadness. Only in the last decades of life can we stand—at least so I have come to believe—in the exact space between generations; only then have we earned the right to celebrate our citizenship on that precise threshold.

THE FAMILY LOST
AND FOUND

I am all the daughters of my father's house.

—SHAKESPEARE, *Twelfth Night*

IN THE EARLY DAYS of this women's movement, someone originated the idea that women in a group identify themselves by their name, continuing: daughter of (mother), daughter of (grandmother), and so on. It was soon noted how few women could go back beyond their grandmothers; the female line seemed to have vanished from the female memory. I could not name my female forebears beyond my maternal grandmother, although my daughter Emily was able to announce herself as the eldest daughter of an eldest daughter (me: I was an only child) of an eldest daughter of an eldest daughter. We both felt that to be a proud heritage, comparable to the ancient benediction of being the seventh son of a seventh son, though less often noticed.

A woman's search for female progenitors, and for female family members bearing news of other women, though it may always have been a strong desire, became even more pronounced with the rise of contemporary feminism. The last years have seen many books about newly discovered grandmothers, aunts, great-grandmothers—brave women who vanished, unrecorded by male historians of the family and much else.

I was in my sixties when I discovered that there were generations of women in my father's family I had never heard of, never known. My mother's family had provided me with a loved grandmother (run over by a car when I was ten) and five aunts, all close to me when I was young, the youngest only thirteen years older than I. Of my father's family I knew nothing, not even that he had three older sisters, all of whom were merely prologue to the birth, finally, of a son, my father.

Which was stranger: that I never knew my father's family, or that I never wondered why I did not know them? My mother's family sufficed—it was large; it surrounded, sometimes even engulfed, my childhood; and my father seemed, if I thought about it at all, a part of that maternal clan. And so, when I had left Columbia, when that departure was recorded in the press and the names of my mother and father were mentioned, I heard from a complex of relatives altogether new to me. One had known of scattered European families miraculously reunited, sometimes years later, after World War II. My family was lost to me within the bounds of New York State.

Yes, but . . . of course I had known in a general way of their existence. My mother had occasionally mentioned my father's mother with disdain, even with contempt. Since my father seemed to concur in this judgment, I never questioned it, apparently long satisfied with the explanation that she was ignorant, perhaps crazy, and spoke little English. I knew when she died, because my father went to her funeral rather than to his office; my mother did not accompany him. Why did I not then ask more about that grandmother? Later, when I was a married adult, I did learn more—not about my father's mother, but about his oldest sister, whom he had, before undergoing an operation, asked me to care for should he not survive; he survived, and the matter was not mentioned again.

It was, therefore, only when I had passed fifty and was in the midst of relishing my year at the Radcliffe (later the Bunting) Institute, that I began to think about my father's family at all, ask him some questions about them, and piece together what I could gather from his brief family narrative.

The book that emerged from that Radcliffe year, *Reinventing Womanhood,* represented, in its introduction, what was for me a remarkable act of bravery; it still seems brave to me upon reflection. In this current age of memoirs, detailed recollections, and the publication of one's most personal ordeals and imaginings, my need of the courage required to speak personally and of my family in the late 1970s must seem quixotic, if not deluded.

I had been trained, in my graduate years, to regard the personal as inadmissible in any work of criticism, certainly in any literary analysis of texts. For a woman like me fighting her way up the slippery academic ladder, to suggest a connection between life and literature would have been madness. Indeed, it was even inadvisable to proclaim one's womanhood. Therefore, it was only in 1977 that I recognized the inadequacy, the falsity, of speaking as a woman critic in the established impersonal male mode of objective fiats delivered as from an Olympian committee. If I wished to speak about "womanhood," and I did, I was obviously obliged to speak as a woman, to claim authority for my individual viewpoint, and thus to take the terrible risk of revealing my experience and my personal history. I think I have never done anything harder: not only was my entire literary education opposed to such self-revelation, but I was, by nature and upbringing, private.

In *Reinventing Womanhood* therefore, I reported, among other intimate (as it seemed to me then) items, what I knew of my father's family, of himself as the prized "boy," born after three sisters, the two eldest of whom, preceding him and his mother to America, had enabled him to arrive, an immigrant age four, at Ellis Island. I thought through the years of those first frightened girls, my father's sisters Fanny and Molly, twelve and fourteen, coming alone to this unknown country, whose language they could not speak, to earn the passage money for the rest of their family. Surely they must have been frightened. Even now, I find it difficult to grasp what that task required of them in the way of courage and determination. They earned money sewing for the Manhattan Shirt Company, starting each at the wage of $2.50 a week. From this they saved enough for tickets to be sent back to the old country for their mother and brother and the third sister. Fanny and Molly supported the five of them until my father took over the entire family responsibility when he was fourteen. My father, as though he had just remembered it in connection with the account of his immigration, told me the story of the youngest sister (whose name he never mentioned), who had been very bright, whom a teacher had tried to rescue but had finally abandoned the attempt after failing to communicate with the ignorant, fearful mother who spoke hardly any English, and the small boy who seemed the head of the family. I gathered that my father, the male, was the hope of the family, its center and its authority.

Thirteen years after the publication of *Reinventing Womanhood,* I resigned from Columbia. My departure from the University after thirty-three years of teaching there provoked the press coverage that would reunite me with my father's lost relatives. Within weeks, they had written to me: the family was, of course, in no sense lost, except to me.

The first letter was from the son of Fanny, the oldest sister, of whom my father had first spoken to me at the time of his operation. This cousin, Herbert, wrote that he had pictures of my father's mother and father and of my father as a dignified young man. (In this latter picture I knew, as soon as Herbert showed it to me, that my father could not be older than sixteen, despite the high starched collar and the formal look, because he grew a mustache at seventeen in order to pass for twenty-one. He bears a remarkable resemblance to my son at the same age, despite *his* long hair and casual demeanor.) My cousin wrote: "My Uncle Archie was very good to me when I was a boy; what I owe him can't be repaid, but it can be passed on." This was my father's byword, and it became mine. Nevertheless, we both, I suspect, while not anticipating reciprocity, secretly hoped for it and occasionally received it, to our happy astonishment.

Herbert turned out (how remarkable are genes) to be, like me, the writer of several series of mystery novels, the earliest of which features a detective named Alexander Gold; my father's name was Archibald Gold ("Archibald" once he had arrived in America—whatever his name may have been in Lithuania—after Teddy Roosevelt's son, or so my father's mother told him and he me, when I inquired about his fancy name). Herbert's are cerebral mysteries, classic puzzles of the locked room, Freeman Wills Crofts genre, but with delightful dialogue and interchange. Another series features a detective named Ed Baer whose Jewish humor is both familiar and unexpected, leading one critic quoted on the jacket to insist that even his gentile friends will enjoy it. (Recently, Herbert coauthored a detective novel with Ed Koch.) A civil engineer before his retirement, Herbert had in addition (in the coincidence rather than gene department) been project manager of the East Campus complex at Columbia University. His son-in-law, it subsequently transpired, is a Distinguished Professor at the CUNY graduate center and well known to my many friends who teach there.

My husband and I soon met Herbert and his remarkable wife, Melly, exactly my age. Melly is a tall woman, considerably taller than her husband, who, proud of that, has given his detective Ed Baer a tall, perceptive wife. Melly had been born in Munich, remembered Kristallnacht (1938), and had escaped with her parents and brother to the United States as a fifteen-year-old. Her father died, two years after the family's arrival in this country, from injuries suffered in a concentration camp; Melly went to work at sixteen, as did her younger brother when he reached that age. At twenty, her brother began his professional career, teaching at a number of universities and ending up as a professor at a Massachusetts university, a specialist in Yeats, a poet I also regularly taught. (*His* son is on the foreign desk at *The New York Times*.) Melly at twenty wanted only to begin a family, to replace the one lost in Germany. She received her college degree many years later, and eventually became a teacher of English. Her intelligence and acerbic wit attracted me, as did the fact that she was less conservative than Herbert, who, like my father, is firmly conservative and a despiser of modern art. Melly told me that my father had paid for her and Herbert's honeymoon at a time not too distant from my own marriage; my father had never mentioned this, nor the fact I only now learned—that he had paid the tuition at Cooper Union, enabling Herbert to become an engineer.

The next letter was from the daughter of my father's youngest sister, whose name I now learned was Mary. Two years younger than I, this cousin had apparently been named Carolyn because it was my name, so my father's sisters must have known something of us, his other remote family. Carolyn told me that Herbert had been his grandmother Rebecca's favorite; my father had, inevitably, been her favorite child.

In almost the next mail, I heard from my oldest living cousin, Muriel, the eldest of Mary's six daughters, as Carolyn had been the youngest. Mary's husband had died when she was still pregnant with her Carolyn, and my father had sent Mary a weekly sum of money. Muriel, eighty years old, wrote: "I always wanted to thank Uncle Archie for all he did for [us] over the years. When I went into the city I would stand on Madison Avenue near his office, but I never got up the courage to go upstairs and see him. I was afraid he would think I was looking for help again." This was a blow to my sixty-six-year-old spirit: I was glad he had helped them, but somehow his generosity seemed . . . well, I asked myself, what did it seem? If he could not offer them love, or even recognition, he could offer financial support. That is surely better than nothing, is it not?

Muriel wrote again: "Momma never knew their real name [the name of the family in Russia]—just that it had been changed to Gold [by the immigration officer]. I wished I had coaxed more family history from Momma and Tante Molly. They didn't like to talk about 'old times' mostly because it stigmatized them as 'immigrants.' " Mary, like my father, had abandoned Judaism, and had, like her sisters, married a gentile. I learned that Molly, my father's middle sister, had moved to California, where her descendants still lived, out of touch with the rest of the family.

And then there appeared a letter from Brian, a fourth relative, this one the age of my oldest child; his mother had also been one of Mary's six daughters. He had discovered his mother's Jewish ancestry only recently, and wrote to me of it: "[Your] publicity has opened another door for me into the ancestry of my mother and the origins of her spirit, her intelligence and her anger as a woman in a man's world. My mother passed away fourteen years ago shortly after I came to live in New York City. It is one of my greatest sorrows that I was not able to love her and appreciate her for the influence and leadership she brought to my life when she was alive." Brian's mother had served in the Army during World War II, and then, like Rosie the Riveter, returned to the female destiny demanded in the fifties.

By this time Carolyn had written again to tell me more about the family. Of the six sisters, four survive and two, she and Muriel, are widows. Between them, they had produced nine offspring, adopted one, married eleven times, divorced six. And she ended with a story that she thought I, as a feminist, "might find interesting."

"At the close of the war [for Carolyn's and my generation 'the' war is always World War II] I was working for the Prudential Insurance Company at the home office in downtown Newark and attending evening college classes nearby. Because of the manpower shortage, the Pru had suspended its policy of firing women when they married, but the status of women in the company was low. Several of the men in my department were also attending classes after work and these men were excused from overtime. I was not, so I quit. I was nineteen years old."

In time I met all the cousins who had written. One snowy day, my husband and I went to Long Island, together with Brian, his wife Chris, and their baby Hannah, to meet Muriel and Carolyn, the oldest and youngest of Mary's daughters. Muriel had just earned her G.E.D., the high school equivalency degree, and was planning to go to college. Wonderfully vital, funny, and smart at eighty, she had been eager when young to continue her education, but had been forced, by her mother, Mary, to go to work at fourteen to help support the fatherless family. She intended now to pursue the course denied her both when she was young, and when she was a wife and mother.

I met all these remarkable people in my sixties, and wished I had known them through the years. I found the women cousins gallant and feisty and risk-taking, although some of their sisters had suffered deeply from depression and despair; one had committed suicide. Their courage, humor, and lack of self-pity were notable. From my father's sisters, Fanny and Molly, who had found the fortitude to come as girls to America, to the youngest of the grandchildren, Carolyn, who had the guts, long before this feminist movement, to walk out of a job because she was discriminated against as a woman, these women had been brave and ambitious, and must, I thought, have nurtured wild desires for something beyond the conventional lives allowed them. And I took special pleasure in the fact that my cousin Herbert had married a woman of high intelligence, daring, and courage. Melly, while only a cousin by marriage, is marked by the same early frustration, the same subsequent boldness and determination. You, she has said to me, were a princess. Hardly, I think, remembering the "princesses" I despised, and my own refusal ever to dress properly, my never having been, as princesses are, indulged.

I believe that I inherited, through my father, the hopes of his sisters and female cousins. Yet I had my father's support in everything I wished to undertake, even though his views were so conservative. Recently, someone asked me if I believed he would have been so supportive had I had a brother. This question, oddly enough, was a profound shock to this sixty-something-year-old woman. I felt myself react to it as those with cardiac arrest respond to the powerful electrical impulse shot through their body to revive them. I now had to see the truth. I was the only child he had, and he offered me what support he could, keeping me from the family that had so inhibited the possibilities of his sisters and, it must have seemed, of their daughters. I had the education Mary never got; I attended the sort of college Muriel and Melly could only dream of; he had paid for Melly's honeymoon, but not for her education—perhaps such an idea had never occurred to him or her or Herbert. I had to recognize that being an only child was all that had saved me from being a princess, however royally fortunate my life must have appeared to Melly. A brother would have pushed me into a stereotypically female role; I would have been the sister, educated, of course, but not expected to insist upon a professional career or revolutionary opinions. This was a shocking truth to have to face in one's sixties, but a salubrious one. To reconsider one's life, seeing it suddenly in a new formation, may be a tremor worth undergoing in one's later years.

Now, in finding this lost family, I found a rare female inheritance. Can I doubt today that my father's constant encouragement of me even when our political views veered widely and disruptively apart had become a way to repay the larger debt he must have felt he owed his sisters?

In his generation, and particularly in the Jewish Orthodox religion, all the effort, the encouragement, the affirmation of ambition, went to the males. Perhaps for some Orthodox Jews it still does. Meeting my cousins showed me, in a more personal and dramatic way than I had previously confronted as a feminist, how great a price such women and their mothers paid as "disposable" women, and how committed we must be in "passing on" what they have given, rewarding their effort and their disappointment with the rights of later generations of women.

Had these brave women whispered to me over the years when I guessed, long before this women's movement and despite my own privileged life, the constraint on women's destinies and the privileges of males who deprive their sisters of scope and opportunity? Had these "lost" relatives of mine tinged my life with a sense of their deprivations and hopes, or had this knowledge that made me so early a feminist been passed on to me more directly by my father, because I was an only child and in acknowledgement of the degree to which his sisters and their daughters had been defrauded?

I was fortunate that happenstance brought these women to me. But once they were there, I thought that one could do worse in one's sixties than to search out family women of earlier generations who might, if one could learn about them, offer examples of courage and gallant, if hidden, lives. Following families into the past, thence into the present, as I was permitted to do, offers a sense of hope, no matter how lonely or isolated one's life as a woman has seemed. In my own case, whatever the source of my early commitment to changing women's lives, it seemed to me as I met this "lost family" that the message about the necessity to expand the restricted lives of women, the message I had never, from girlhood on, been able to ignore, had, suddenly and wonderfully, assumed human form.

ON MORTALITY

When I am dead, my dearest,
    Sing no sad songs for me;
Plant thou no roses at my head,
    Nor shady cypress tree:
Be the green grass above me
    With showers and dewdrops wet:
And if thou wilt, remember,
    And if thou wilt, forget.

I shall not see the shadows,
    I shall not feel the rain;
I shall not hear the nightingale
    Sing on as if in pain:
And dreaming through the twilight
    That does not rise nor set,
Haply I may remember,
    And haply may forget.

—CHRISTINA ROSSETTI, "Song"

CHRISTINA ROSSETTI wrote of death when she was young and yet, with the imagination of a poet and, perhaps more significantly, the desperation of a confined young woman with no clear or attractive destiny before her, she had a premature sense of the ultimate indifference of the dead. The dead may be, as Rossetti believed, indifferent, but I, still living, must not allow myself to succumb to indifference's seduction; however often apathy assaults me in these last decades, I know it to be dangerous. I have found that detachment serves me only insofar as it encourages me, both to resist foretelling doom upon a world I cannot really know or guess at, and to leave the future to those who will inhabit it.

I have been many years learning this. We often hear the story of the person who plants a tree under whose shade he or she will never sit, but we who are near the end of our lives must also, I feel certain, have confidence in the quality of that shade. The world may, as Rossetti suggests, indifferently view my own departure; dead, what shall I know? But until death, I hope to abjure the indifference that is prompted by a perception of the future as degenerative.

I am sharply aware that people do, more and more often these days, live past eighty, and many of them are reported to live productive, satisfying lives. But many more fall into indifference. Writing in *The New York Times Magazine,* Michael Norman described the life of his eighty-eight-year-old aunt. "It's no good," he reported her as saying. "I'm living too long already. What's the point?"

This harsh question, "What's the point?," is judged by some as cruel, unacceptable in our culture. To me, it is a very real question, the question that renders living too long dangerous, lest we live past both the right point and our chance to die. As I have admitted, I was, at the end of my sixties, "half in love with easeful death"—to borrow Keats's lovely phrase—turning every consciously considered moment of life into a balance: life or death. Or, as Emily Dickinson imagined it:

> Because I could not stop for Death—
> He kindly stopped for me—
> The carriage held but just Ourselves—
> And Immortality.
>
> We slowly drove—He knew no haste
> And I had put away
> My Labor and my leisure too,
> For His Civility.

In my sixties, I found that death adds the intensity that used, I imagine, to come with the parting of friends and lovers in the days before direct communication over distances was possible, when even mail took many weeks to wend its way across oceans and continents. Those of whatever age who have been near death tell us that life, when they returned to it, was never again the same. I think that that same intensity, that constant awareness of newness and brightness, is also possible in one's sixties and after; it certainly has been in mine. Perhaps only when we know on our pulses (another phrase of Keats's) that our time is limited do we properly treasure it.

For Harold Nicolson's seventieth birthday, his friends gave him and his wife, Vita Sackville-West, a boat trip to Java. The two occupied separate cabins, each working on his or her next book. As an epigraph to *Journey to Java,* his account of the trip, Nicolson used one of Montaigne's pithy observations:

Above all, now that I feel my life to be brief in time, do I seek to extend it in weight. I try to delay the velocity of its flight by the velocity with which I grasp it; and to compensate for the speed of its collapse by the zest which I throw into it. The shorter my hold on life, the deeper and fuller do I seek to render it. Others feel the sweetness of contentment and well-being; I feel it just as much as they do, but not by letting it just slip away.

This sense of limited time has given me, rather to my surprise, what I have come to understand is an eccentric, delicate distinction between my love for my children and for my grandchildren. Grandchildren have always been praised to me as the ultimate in parenthood, the joy of young children without the responsibility: one hugs them, plays with them, and hands them back. Our children's children say to us: I continue. But I have not found the joy in my grandchildren, great as it is, half so profound as the pleasure I take in my adult children. To perceive the enchantment of small children does not require the eyes of the old. To taste with special relish the conversation of one's grown-up children does, I suspect, demand a special sense of present time, a sense pertinent only to those in their sixties, or so it seems to me. I shall not see my grandchildren grow into adults, and if I were to last that long, I doubt I would retain as fervent an interest in them, their opinions, their experiences, as I now enjoy in colloquy with my own adult children. Perhaps because I am not a natural lover of children, the most potent reward for parenthood I have known has been delight in my fully grown progeny. They are friends with an extra dimension of affection. True, there is also an extra dimension of resentment on the children's part, but once offspring are in their thirties, their ability to love their parents, perhaps in contemplation of the deaths to come, expands, and, if one is fortunate, grudges recede.

I have been intrigued in recent years to read the many compelling memoirs that are being written about dead parents. My friend Nancy Miller has published a book on this subject, *Bequests and Betrayals;* she once thought of calling it "Necessary Betrayals." Her point is not only that the children betray the parents in writing of them, but that the parents have sometimes betrayed the children in withholding certain truths. Miller's examples include Susan Cheever, writing about her father, John Cheever; Art Spiegelman, writing about his father in *Maus;* Simone de Beauvoir, writing about her mother in *A Very Easy Death.* Miller is acutely aware of both her own and

Beauvoir's childlessness, a condition that makes the death of a parent especially poignant. I, meanwhile, have become tantalized by the question of how, as the parent of grown children, one estimates them in view of one's own death. I view my children as a source, not of personal immortality but of personal pleasure, personal satisfaction. And because I will die before many years are past, those satisfactions have a piercing beauty. If grandchildren are my future, if I am entranced, as certainly I am, in watching life once again develop in them, I nonetheless know that, as I watch, my life slips away. With my adult children, as with work and companionship, life is grasped, the rendering is deep and full.

But though I viewed my death as welcome in my sixties, and only the fear of being held captive in a long illness, or reaching the time of feeling, like Michael Norman's aunt, "I'm living too long already, What's the point?" fills me with deep anxiety and dread, I do not contemplate the death of my husband with the same equanimity. Indeed, I do not allow myself to think of it at all. Death as a friend is all very well for oneself. I like to quote Stevie Smith:

> Why do I think of Death
> As a friend?
> It is because he is a scatterer,
> He scatters the human frame
> The nerviness and the great pain,
> Throws it on the fresh fresh air

And now it is nowhere.
Only sweet death does this,
Sweet Death, kind Death,
Of all the gods you are best.

But you, death, are the best god only for myself. Therein lies the ultimate irony. I would not, of course, want my husband to linger unhappily with some illness, but I refuse to accept the thought that he will not, in exactly the condition he is in now, outlive me. I know that women are expected to outlive men, but we are close in age, and his mother lived into her ninety-eighth year. His grandmother, dying at ninety-three, was half as old as the United States; she had been to school in Cincinnati with William Howard Taft, whom they called "Fatty" even then, and she remembered the assassination of Lincoln. I take these facts as his promise to outlive me. And, it need hardly be affirmed, the young must never die. I have lost, in addition to Helen from suicide, a student, a close friend younger than I, and a friend my age from cancer. I cannot contemplate any more deaths of those not yet past sixty, although I recognize the hubris in announcing that, and I do not wish to tempt the gods with my wishes for immunity. (When I am not, with May Sarton, half believing in guardian angels, I follow the Greek attitudes toward fate; they knew best, I believe, how life goes.)

Perhaps death, the nearness of it, transforms long marriages, as indeed it seems to do, when the partners are in their sixties. I have noticed that marriages that have endured over many decades seem to have earned, as reward, a mutual mellowness. For me, to speak of marriage is to speak of husbands. True, there are long relationships between two women or two men, but they have left us few accounts; nor have we made more than feeble attempts to understand their condition and speak to it. Women historians are only now making these stories known to us. In *My Partner and I: Molly Dewson, Feminism, and New Deal Politics,* Susan Ware has recounted the history of Dewson and her lasting relationship with her partner, Polly Porter. Molly Dewson, feminist and political "boss," worked, after much earlier political experience, with Eleanor Roosevelt in Al Smith's unsuccessful presidential campaign, and in Franklin Roosevelt's successful one. But in 1938, when Dewson was serving on the three-member Social Security Board in Washington, she resigned her position after nine months because of the strain it was causing to her partnership with Porter. That relationship endured for fifty-two years until Dewson's death in 1962.

Then there is Sylvia Townsend Warner, writing of her love for Valentine Ackland, her lifelong companion, to a man fearing to lose his lover: "Here I am," she comforted him, "grey as a badger, wrinkled as a walnut, and never a beauty at my best; but here I sit, and yonder sits the other one, who had all the cards in her hand—except one. That I was better at loving and being loved." And, of course, there is the uniquely famous relationship of Gertrude Stein and Alice Toklas.

But though accounts of such long partnerships are rare, an honest account by a woman of her marriage and of the husband she has cherished, endured, and threatened to abandon over many years is rarest of all. Why do long marriages occasionally endow their inhabitants with a rare kind of equilibrium otherwise almost unknown in human relations? My guess is that the value of the moment has at last overshadowed the long history of resentments, betrayals, and boredom. Many husbands, many men, are boring, certainly more boring than women, though no woman would ever dream of telling them so. I, like many women, was for long capable, at some act of thoughtlessness or forgetfulness on my husband's part, of allowing that one sin of omission to serve as a mental magnet, attracting to it many other occasions when one's temper was tried almost beyond endurance. For some reason, at least in my experience and the experience of those who discuss this with me, men do not seem to cherish quite so pristine a backlog of episodes evoking resentment; their memory of emotional moments, good or bad, at least if they are not writers, is frail. But in my sixties, this rush of memory and anger receded, indeed quite dissipated itself. Anger in my sixties, rare enough, was anger at the present moment, and did not reach beyond it, into either the past or the future.

The impression I have, therefore, of marriage in my sixties is of a time when I took to living only for the moment—when, above all, I took to expecting nothing that long years of close association had by now, at long last, assured me would never occur. He would not change his personality or his habits of loving, and neither would I. I took a hint from George Balanchine, a man whose achievements had figured prominently in my husband's and my long life together (my husband has been a ballet devotee almost as long as we have been married). Balanchine said:

I like now. So many people I know want always to remember things. . . . Everything in the past is the same to me, I don't care about it. I like now.

Balanchine also said: "Just dance the steps." Meaning, I suppose, that dancers ought not to worry about the whole ballet, its meaning, its significance, but should—just dance the steps. That is what I have come to believe that awareness of mortality has taught me, particularly about marriage.

And now that I have got used to my husband, expecting neither more nor less than who he is, now that I know he will never become a poet of love, or be likely to remember what I said yesterday as readily as he recalls what hotel he stayed at in a foreign city decades ago, I have found life good, and I do not accept the possibility of his desertion. What would happen should I desert him is—is it not?—his problem, one I doubt he spends much time contemplating; abstract questions have never intrigued him.

The poet Jane Kenyon, who died of leukemia at
the age of forty-nine, wrote this poem, "Otherwise." I
suspect it was written with her illness in mind. I read
it as appropriate to one's sixties and beyond.

> I got out of bed
> on two strong legs.
> It might have been
> otherwise. I ate
> cereal, sweet
> milk, ripe, flawless
> peach. It might
> have been otherwise.
> I took a dog uphill
> to the birch wood.
> All morning I did
> the work I love.
>
> At noon I lay down
> with my mate. It might
> have been otherwise.
> We ate dinner together
> at a table with silver
> candlesticks. It might
> have been otherwise.
> I slept in a bed
> in a room with paintings
> on the walls, and
> planned another day
> just like this day.
> But one day, I know,
> it will be otherwise.

Notes

PREFACE

1 "Since [nature] has fitly planned": *Cicero: De Senectute.*

5 "Apparently [Larkin] is sixty": Alan Bennett, *Writing Home,* p. 320.

5 "Every word of praise": Andrew Motion, *Philip Larkin: A Writer's Life,* p. 495.

5 "that hulking milestone of mortality": William Styron, *Darkness Visible: A Memoir of Madness,* p. 78.

5 "My old friends": Marilyn Hacker, "Against Elegies," in *Winter Numbers.*

6 "I answered spontaneously": May Sarton, *At Seventy,* p. 10.

10 "The readiness forms in waves": Käthe Kollwitz, as quoted in Martha Kearns, *Käthe Kollwitz: Woman and Artist,* p. 166.

THE SMALL HOUSE

11 Epigraph: W. H. Auden, "Thanksgiving for a Habitat," in *About the House.*

11 "If to be left": Edna St. Vincent Millay, Sonnet XLIV.

THE DOG WHO CAME TO STAY

25 Epigraph: Poem "by" Arthur Miller's dog Lola, "Lola's Lament," in *Unleashed: Poems by Writers' Dogs.*

30 "Day after day": Rudyard Kipling, "Four Feet," in *Rudyard Kipling's Verse: The Definitive Edition.*

TIME

37 Epigraph: Adrienne Rich, "Prospective Immigrants Please Note," in *Collected Early Poems: 1950–1970.*

38 "All the things I most disliked": Doris Grumbach, *Extra Innings: A Memoir,* p. 287.

41 "When you speak, sweet,": William Shakespeare, *The Winter's Tale,* IV, iv: 136–146.

44 "I think as one grows older": Sylvia Townsend Warner, *Letters,* pp. 267–268.

46 "explaining that he had now mapped": Nora Sayre, *Previous Convictions: A Journey Through the 1950s,* p. 72.

47 "I am convinced": William James, as quoted in Gay Wilson Allen, *William James: A Biography,* p. 437.

53 "The essential in a biography": Warner, *Letters,* p. 226.

54 "One has a dozen motives": Ibid.

54 "I woke up *knowing*": *The Diaries of Sylvia Townsend Warner,* p. 251.

55 "In the evening": Ibid, p. 280.

E-MAIL

57 Epigraph: Oscar Wilde, *The Importance of Being Earnest.*

A UNIQUE PERSON

69 Epigraph: Robert Mezey, afterword to *Ants on the Melon*, by Virginia Hamilton Adair.

70 "If I accepted invitations": May Sarton, *Plant Dreaming Deep*, p. 92.

75 "We have to make myths": Ibid, p. 185.

83 Sarton's loss of "self": May Sarton, *After the Stroke*, p. 18.

83 "a leap into old age": Ibid, p. 35.

84 "The wish to die is staggering": May Sarton, *At Eighty-two*, p. 306.

86 "there is something wrong when solitude": *Journal of a Solitude*, pp. 122–123.

86 On Sarton and movies: Ibid, pp. 82, 138.

86 "I may die within the next few days": *Encore: A Journal of the Eightieth Year*, p. 271.

ENGLAND

89 Epigraph: Marianne Moore, "England," in *Collected Poems*.

92 "never heard of the bloody woman": Hermione Lee, *Virginia Woolf*, p. 772.

101 "At twenty we find our friends": W. H. Auden, from his dedication to *City Without Walls*.

SEX AND ROMANCE

103 Epigraph: Hermione Lee, *Willa Cather: Double Lives*, p. 111.

104 "The only man who proposed to her": Kate Muir, review of *Desert Queen* by Janet Wallace, *New York Times Book Review*, 9/8/96.

106 "reading two books simultaneously": Selina Hastings,

review of *Desert Queen* by Janet Wallace, *New Yorker*, 9/30/96.

108 "I'm sick, she said to herself": Doris Lessing, *Love, Again*, pp. 126–127.

108 "I thought I had had a happy life": Marilyn French, *My Summer with George*, p. 77.

111 "She could marry James de Witt": P. D. James, *Original Sin*, p. 71.

MEMORY

115 Epigraph: Edward Fitzgerald, *The Rubáiyát of Omar Khayyám.*

123 "Tears, idle tears": Alfred, Lord Tennyson, "Tears, Idle Tears."

ON NOT WEARING DRESSES

125 Epigraph: Susan Brownmiller, *Femininity*, p. 66.

129 "Because I don't like this artificial gender distinction.": Ibid, p. 81.

134 Marjorie Garber on androgyny: Marjorie Garber, *Vice Versa: Bisexuality and the Eroticism of Everyday Life.*

UNMET FRIENDS

137 Epigraph: Maxine Kumin, "Notes on a Blizzard," in *Our Ground Time Here Will Be Brief.*

141 "I began as a poet": All Maxine Kumin prose quotations are from the section "interviews" in *To Make a Prairie: Essays on Poets, Poetry, and Country Living*, pp. 3–65.

142 "part of my life back": Maxine Kumin, "Address to the Angels," in *Our Ground Time.*

143 Maxine Kumin on early poetry at Radcliffe: Kumin, *Prairie*, p. 18.

144 "All day I watch": Maxine Kumin, "Notes on a Blizzard."

144 "The Day / of infamy": Maxine Kumin, "Remembering Pearl Harbor at the Tutankhamen Exhibit," in *Our Ground Time.*

145 "The woman who needs to create": May Sarton, *Mrs. Stevens Hears the Mermaids Singing.*

145 "I'm afraid I don't agree": Maxine Kumin, *Prairie*, p. 52.

146 "androgynous pagan muse": Maxine Kumin, *Women, Animals, and Vegetables,* p. 19.

146 "Whoever mows with a big machine": Maxine Kumin, "Distance," in *Selected Poems 1960–1990.*

146 "programmed into one kind of life": Maxine Kumin, *Prairie*, p. 31.

148 "Sleeping with animals": Maxine Kumin, "Sleeping with Animals," in *Selected Poems 1960–1990.*

149 "Around me old friends": Maxine Kumin, "Distance," in *Selected Poems 1960–1990.*

151 "Do not snub me with silence": Vanessa Bell, *Selected Letters,* p. 445.

154 "*Please* don't write a life": Sylvia Townsend Warner, *Letters,* p. 120.

154 "She loved, and needed": Claire Harman, *Sylvia Townsend Warner: A Biography,* p. 309.

155 "a correspondence kept up": Sylvia Townsend Warner, as quoted in Harman, *STW*, p. 309.

LISTENING TO THE YOUNG(ER)

157 Epigraph: Lewis Carroll, *Alice's Adventures in Wonderland.*

159 "one really charming quality": Marilyn French, *My Summer with George,* p. 217.

160 "What I understand by manners": Lionel Trilling, *The Liberal Imagination,* p. 203.

161 "What with one thing and another": Virginia Woolf, *To the Lighthouse,* p. 35.

LIVING WITH MEN

165 Epigraph: Dorothy L. Sayers, *Busman's Honeymoon.*

167 On Rosalind Franklin: Anne Sayre, *Rosalind Franklin and DNA.*

SADNESS

177 Epigraph: Shakespeare, *The Merchant of Venice,* I, 1–7.

THE FAMILY LOST AND FOUND

191 Epigraph: Shakespeare, *Twelfth Night,* II, iv: 119.

ON MORTALITY

205 Epigraph: Christina Rossetti, "Song."

206 "It's no good": Michael Norman, "Living Too Long," *New York Times Magazine,* 1/14/96.

207 "Because I could not stop for Death": Emily Dickinson, "Because I Could Not Stop for Death."

208 "Above all, now that I feel my life": Montaigne, *Essays,* III, xiii.

210 "Why do I think of Death": Stevie Smith, "Why Do I Think . . . ," in *The Collected Poems of Stevie Smith.*

212 On Molly Dewson and Polly Porter: Susan Ware, *My*

Partner and I: Molly Dewson, Feminism, and New Deal Politics.

212 "Here I am": Sylvia Townsend Warner, *Letters,* pp. 129–130.

214 "I like now.": George Balanchine, as quoted in Barbara Newman, "Returning for Balanchine," *Ballet Review,* Winter 1993, p. 75.

215 "I got out of bed": Jane Kenyon, "Otherwise," in *Otherwise: New & Selected Poems.*

GRATEFUL ACKNOWLEDGMENT is made to the following publishers for permission to reprint selected materials: "Against Elegies," from *Winter Numbers* by Marilyn Hacker. Copyright 1994 by Marilyn Hacker. Reprinted by permission of W. W. Norton & Company, Inc.; "Thanksgiving for a Habitat," from *About the House* by W. H. Auden. Copyright 1965 by W. H. Auden. Reprinted by permission of Random House; "Lola's Lament," from *Unleashed: Poems by Writers' Dogs* by Amy Hempel and Jim Shepard. Copyright 1995 by Amy Hempel and Jim Shepard. Reprinted by permission of Crown Publishers, Inc.; "Prospective Immigrants Please Note," from *Collected Early Poems: 1950–1970* by Adrienne Rich. Copyright 1963, 1967, 1993 by Adrienne Rich. Reprinted by permission of the author and W. W. Norton & Company, Inc.; lines from *Extra Innings* by Doris Grumbach. Copyright 1993 by Doris Grumbach. Reprinted by permission of W. W. Norton & Company, Inc.; lines from *The Letters of Sylvia Townsend Warner,* ed. William Maxwell. Copyright 1982 by William Maxwell. Reprinted by permission of Viking; lines from *William James: A Biography* by Gay Wilson Allen. Copyright 1967 by Gay Wilson Allen. Reprinted by permission of Viking; lines from Robert Mezey's Afterword to *Ants on the Melon* by Virginia Hamilton Adair. Copyright 1996 by Virginia Hamilton Adair. Reprinted by permission of Random House; lines from *My Summer with George* by Marilyn French. Copyright 1996 by Marilyn French. Reprinted by permission of Alfred A. Knopf; lines from *Femininity* by Susan Brownmiller. Copyright 1984 by Susan Brownmiller. Reprinted by permission of Simon & Schuster; "Notes on a Blizzard" from *Our Ground Time Here Will Be Brief* by Maxine Kumin. Copyright 1982 by Maxine Kumin. Reprinted by permission of the author; lines from *To Make a Prairie: Essays on Poets, Poetry, and Country Living* by Maxine Kumin. Copyright 1979 by Maxine Kumin. Reprinted by permission of University of Michigan Press; "Sleeping with Animals" and "Distance," from *Selected Poems 1960–1990* by Maxine Kumin. Copyright 1989 by Maxine Kumin. Reprinted by permission of W. W. Norton & Company, Inc.; lines from *The Selected Letters of Vanessa Bell,* edited by Regina Marler. Copyright 1993 by Regina Marler. Reprinted by permission of Pantheon; "Why Do I Think. . . ," from *The Collected Poems of Stevie Smith* by Stevie Smith. Copyright 1976 by Stevie Smith. Reprinted by permission of Penguin UK; "Otherwise," from *Otherwise: New & Selected Poems* by Jane Kenyon. Copyright 1996 by Jane Kenyon. Reprinted by permission of Graywolf Press, Saint Paul, Minnesota; lines from *Cicero: De Senectute,* translated by William Armstead Falconer, reprinted by permission of Harvard University Press and the Loeb Classical Library; lines from "England," from *Collected Poems of Marianne Moore.* Copyright by Marianne Moore; Copyright renewed 1963 by Marianne Moore & T. S. Eliot. Reprinted by permission of Simon & Schuster.

© Katy Raddatz

About the Author

Carolyn G. Heilbrun is the author of the now-classic *Writing a Woman's Life, The Education of a Woman: The Life of Gloria Steinem, Toward a Recognition of Androgyny, Reinventing Womenhood,* and other works. She is also the author of the acclaimed Amanda Cross mystery series.